Could You Pass This Test?

TRUE OR FALSE:
* Successful people work the hardest and put in the longest hours.
* The best way to get a job done is to do it yourself.
* You can't work and play at the same time.
* You work best under pressure.
* Managing time means finding ways to save time.

If you said "True" to any of the above you may be your own worst enemy! Here's the book that exposes the facts and fallacies of the marketplace and shows how many of these commonplace myths accepted as fact actually *decrease* your productivity and effectiveness. But more important, WORKING SMART provides the antidote: a surefire way to beat the system before it beats you!

". . . defuses the pervasive myths that hamper effectiveness . . . and presents the antidotes."

—*Kirkus*

". . . simple strategies for increasing one's effective use of time and energy . . . both the workaholic and the procrastinator could benefit from his advice on how to set goals and priorities, cut paperwork, take advantage of teamwork and develop executive ability."

—Publisher's Weekly

Working Smart

How to Accomplish More in Half the Time

Michael LeBoeuf

WARNER BOOKS

A Warner Communications Company

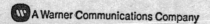

ACKNOWLEDGMENTS

With special thanks to:
Ralph and Lila Stair and Denise Villeré for suggesting
that I write this book.
Merrill Douglass, who influenced many of my ideas
about managing time.
Kathy Matthews for being a guardian angel.
Peggy Tsukahira for a superior editing job.
Fred Hills, Victor de Keyserling and Alice Acheson
for their guidance, ideas and enthusiasm.
Richard Stillman, Maurice Villeré, Cathy Caragliano,
John Dillworth, Lyn Ledbetter, Dean Myrick and
Sherry Snyder for their encouragement and support.
Kathy Ackermann, my typist, for her patience, loyalty
and excellent work.

Contents

Introduction

*"In order that people may be happy in their work,
these three things are needed: They must be fit
for it. They must not do too much of it. And
they must have a sense of success in it."*

—*John Ruskin*

There's just no doubt about it. Most of us work harder than we have to in order to reap the benefits that life has to offer.

That thought crossed my mind some years ago. Feeling that such a thought was hardly unique, I went looking for a book on how to work less and get more done. What did I find? All sorts of interesting self-help books on a multitude of subjects. I read many of them, learning such things as how to intimidate, negotiate and meditate. Others told me how to run, have fun and look out for number one. Still others told me how to live with fear, manage my career and become the greatest thing since bottled beer. "Amazing!" I thought to myself. "Absolutely amazing!"

All of these books helped me in some way, but nowhere could I find a book that directly focused on what

I wanted to know—"How can I get the greatest return on my investment of time and energy?" Or, stated another way, "How can I get more done by spending less of my time and energy?" "Impossible!" you say? Not at all.

Not being able to find a book that answered my question only made me more determined to get some answers. For the past several years, I have been doing research, consulting and conducting seminars teaching people how to make the most of their time and effort.

I have found the following to be our major contributors to failure and fatigue:

1. Unwillingness to invest work in the present for reward in the future. People tend to give up after a halfhearted effort and all efforts toward abandoned goals go for naught.

2. Having programmed, erroneous beliefs about work that we've all been taught.

3. Not knowing or deciding what you want out of life.

4. The inability to manage your time.

5. A life of chaos.

6. A weak self-image, fear of failure, guilt, worry, excessive anger and other irrational time- and energy-draining emotions.

7. Procrastination.

8. The unwillingness or inability to skillfully delegate tasks to others.

9. Communication breakdowns.

10. Unnecessary interpersonal conflicts.

11. Common everyday interruptions such as meetings, visitors and telephone calls.

12. A deluge of paper work.

The causes and cures of each one of these is outlined

step by step in a simple, readable and practical format to make it immediately useful.

If you simply buy this book, read it, put it on the shelf and forget it, I assure you that you won't get your money's worth. However, if you follow the recommendations I am about to give you, this book can represent the beginning of a rewarding growth experience.

First, be an active reader. Read with a pencil or pen in your hand. When you come across a key idea that applies to you, underline it or make notes in the margin. At the end of each chapter make a list of concepts and worksavers that apply to you, and resolve to use them.

Second, don't attempt to make wholesale, abrupt changes in your behavior. You will only find it frustrating and probably unbearable. The best and most lasting way to implement change is gradually, smoothly and systematically. As you compile a list of worksaving ideas, resolve to apply one new idea each week. That may sound terribly slow, but if you do that you will have put over fifty new effectiveness techniques into your life in one year. If you feel it's too slow, try two or three new ideas per week, but back off if you begin to feel uncomfortable.

Finally, don't expect to be perfect. There will be days that you will not or cannot do the things you feel you should or could have done. Some days you simply may not give a damn. Other days, Muphy's Law may rear its ugly head (read Murphy's Law and what to do about it in Chapter 1). No matter what happens, simply resolve to keep trying. Improving your effectiveness is much like playing golf. Theoretically, the perfect golf score is eighteen, but to reach that would mean a hole in one on eighteen consecutive holes. Obviously, no one will ever come anywhere near that. However, this fact doesn't stop millions of avid duffers from trying to improve their score each week. As you strive to work smarter, take a similar approach. Resolve to improve, but realize that this is an area where you will always be able to improve. With that in mind, let's go explode some common work myths. Who knows? It just might take a few strokes off your game.

1
The Effectiveness Plan

CHAPTER 1

Workaholics Unanimous

*"I like my job and am good at it,
but it sure grinds me down sometimes,
and the last thing I need to take home
is a headache."*

—Anacin TV commercial

On a cold, rainy October morning, Edward Kennedy stood by a factory gate seeking votes for the U.S. Senate. As he greeted one elderly worker and asked for his vote, the employee looked at Kennedy and said, "I understand you never worked a day in your life." Before Kennedy had a chance to reply, the worker added, "Well, let me tell you, you haven't missed a damn thing!"

What does work mean to you? Do you think of it as an activity that takes more from you than it gives to you? Do you think of the distinction between play and work as that between pleasure and pain? Do you live to work? Do you work to live? Regardless of your answers one thing is certain: Work is here to stay. By work, I mean the human expenditure of time and energy (both physical and mental) to complete a task. This definition is a very broad one. When you stop and think about it, it means

15

that you spend the overwhelming majority of your waking hours at work. When you brush your teeth, plan a vacation, drive to work or perform household or occupational chores, you are at work. Likewise, you may work at being a better doctor, lawyer, teacher, tennis player, lover or cook. Work, like death and taxes, is an all-encompassing and inescapable reality of life.

Now for the good news. Assembled in the forthcoming pages is a comprehensive set of simple but powerful ideas and techniques that will enable you to conquer your personal energy crisis.

Do you ever feel frustrated and exhausted at the end of the day because you have nothing to show for your efforts? I'll show you some simple ideas that will make every day count and leave you with time and energy to spare.

Do you find yourself rushing to meet deadlines and constantly hassled by an unending stream of crises? I'll give you some ways to beat the deadline hassle and cut down on your firefighting activities.

Is your life one big mass of commitments that leave you feeling confused and immobilized? I'll show you how to organize those commitments, eliminate many and give yourself a feeling of direction.

Do you find yourself feeling guilty about what doesn't get done and worried about what may not get done? I'll convince you that these are useless emotions that only cause you to work more and accomplish less.

Do you find yourself not tackling important projects because they seem overwhelming or unpleasant? I'll explain how you can gain momentum to tackle these projects and follow through to successful completion.

Are you compulsive about having to do everything

yourself? I'll give you some tips on successful delegating.

In working with others, do you often find the going rough due to communication breakdowns and unnecessary conflicts? I'll point out some common pitfalls of communication and conflict and recommend means of avoiding them.

Do you find your work hampered by an unending stream of interruptions such as meetings, visitors and telephone calls? I'll give you some pointers for minimizing them.

Are you drowning in a set of information and paper overload, as most of us are? I'll show you how to quiet the paper tiger down to a mild roar.

To be sure, this is a large order; but I am confident that you will be able to benefit by many, if not all, of the ideas contained here. And the best part is that they are simple, proven and immediately applicable.

EFFECTIVENESS—THE KEY TO IT ALL

As you read this, you may be thinking to yourself that this is a book written by some efficiency nut who wants to turn you into an unfeeling, unthinking automaton. Nothing could be further from the truth.

All too often, many of us confuse effectiveness with efficiency. Being effective is choosing the right goals from a set of alternatives and reaching them. Efficiency, on the other hand, assumes the goals as given and proper and proceeds to find the best means of achieving them. Efficiency is doing the job right, whereas effectiveness is doing the right job. In a nutshell, effectiveness means results. Both are valuable concepts, but in my mind, effectiveness is far more important.

17

TIME—YOUR MOST VALUABLE RESOURCE

What's your time worth? (See Figure 1.) Benjamin Franklin told us that time is money, and in the business sense, this is true. Time is like money in that it is measurable and you can't take it with you. However, as a resource, time has unique properties. We are forced to use time at a constant rate. The inventory is being depleted at an amount of 60 minutes per hour, 24 hours per day, 168 hours per week. Time is irreplaceable. We are all given a finite amount of time, but the irony is that we never know how much we have until it's all gone. Few of us admit to having enough time, but all of us have all that there is; that is the paradox of time. Time is truly our most precious resource.

How old are you? How many more years do you expect to live? When you die, how long will you be dead? I ask these questions not to depress you but rather to impress you with the briefness of our earthly existence. Waste your money and you're only out of money, but waste your time and you've lost a part of your life. Few of us would knowingly take half of our take-home pay and spend it on something that was of absolutely no use to us or anyone else. However, the vast majority of us spend at least fifty percent of each day in various pastimes that provide no earthly use or satisfaction for anyone, including ourselves. We literally waste away half of our lives and do it in oblivious indifference.

Coming to grips with our mortality can help us or hurt us. If we choose to let it hurt us, we can wallow in the futility and tragedy of life. We can conclude that life isn't worth living. Or, as most of us do, we can fool ourselves and believe that our time is infinite, that there

Figure 1 What's Your Time Worth?

if you earn $	every minute is worth	every hour is worth	in a year, one hour a day is worth
$ 2,000	$ .0170	$ 1.02	$ 250
2,500	.0213	1.28	312
3,000	.0256	1.54	375
3,500	.0300	1.79	437
4,000	.0341	2.05	500
5,000	.0426	2.56	625
6,000	.0513	3.07	750
7,000	.0598	3.59	875
7,500	.0640	3.84	937
8,000	.0683	4.10	1,000
8,500	.0726	4.35	1,063
10,000	.0852	5.12	1,250
12,000	.1025	6.15	1,500
14,000	.1195	7.17	1,750
16,000	.1366	8.20	2,000
20,000	.1708	10.25	2,500
25,000	.2135	12.81	3,125
30,000	.2561	15.37	3,750
35,000	.2988	17.93	4,375
40,000	.3415	20.49	5,000
50,000	.4269	25.61	6,250
75,000	.6403	38.42	9,375
100,000	.8523	51.23	12,500

Based on 244 eight-hour working days.

will always be tomorrow to fulfill those lifetime dreams and wishes. Fortunately, there are a few of us who deal with our mortality in a more constructive way. In effect these people say to themselves, "I'm not going to be here forever, so I'd better make the most of every minute, hour, day and year." They view life as a brief but wonderful experience to be enjoyed to the fullest. They live their lives for themselves because they accept the reality that their life is all they have. They accept the responsibility for their own feelings, triumphs and misfortunes. As a result of this take-charge attitude, these persons realize the necessity to plan their lives for maximum personal satisfaction.

In order to make the most of your future time and energy it is imperative that you devote some of your present time and energy to planning. Without sound plans to increase our personal effectiveness most of us tend to drift and stagnate. Some people believe that planning is merely deciding what to do in the future. However, a better definition of planning is deciding what you have to do in order to have a future.

THE INVESTMENT THEORY OF WORK

Simply put, the investment theory of work states that you must be willing to sacrifice some of your present time, energy and short-range satisfactions in order to work less and accomplish more later on.

There is nothing new or earth-shaking about the investment theory of work, and all of us have used it from time to time. When you take a part-time job in addition to your regular duties to save for that new house or car, or when you go back to school for additional or advanced training, you are applying the investment theory.

Most of us, however, don't rely on it systematically as a working principle in our lives. The reason for this is what I call the instant-everything lifestyle. This has become a prevailing norm in our society. Pick up any newspaper, turn on the radio or television, or drive down any suburban highway, and voices from the land of instant everything will announce their readiness to satisfy your every need.

Are you hungry or thirsty? There are fast-food restaurants and express checkout supermarkets by the score. Dislike the way you are? There are literally thousands of establishments crying to make you taller, shorter, lighter, heavier, sexier, healthier, more beautiful and smell better. Want to change your mood? There are pills and potions to pick you up, bring you down, keep you awake and put you to sleep. The list could go on endlessly—it's the incredible miracle of twentieth-century living.

One of the problems with instant everything is that it lulls us into neglecting the future. All that matters is the urgency of satisfying present needs. However, the future is not instant. It runs on a very precise schedule and takes its time getting here. To be sure, tomorrow is promised to no one, but it is also a fact that most of us will be here when it arrives. Fail to control your future and it will control you. Your use of time and energy will be dictated by circumstances rather than by yourself. The relationship of you to time is always one of master to slave. There is no middle ground. The only question is which role you choose to play.

Many of the ideas suggested in this book will at first be unfamiliar and uncomfortable, and involve a greater initial investment of work than do old comfortable habits you have grown accustomed to. However, as the Queen told Alice in Lewis Carroll's *Through the Looking-Glass,* "It's a poor sort of memory that only works backwards." As your "two-way memory" looks forward, you will realize the rewards are indeed greater accomplishment coupled with less devotion of your time and energy.

I happen to be one of those people who believes that

happiness and success don't just happen to someone—they happen when opportunity meets preparation. Those who succeed do so because they were willing to invest in the groundwork and were prepared when the tide of good fortune rolled in.

Working smart requires an investment of thought, self-discipline and change. You must be willing to carefully examine and evaluate your present feelings, values, attitudes and habits about work. Anyone who has ever been faced with the task of an objective self-evaluation will report that it was none too pleasant but terribly enlightening. Once you have completed your self-examination, you must be willing to change your thinking and behavior to that which is more beneficial. Old habits die hard and change is tough. That's why you must discipline yourself until the new behavior becomes old habit. The whole process is one of getting mentally tough with yourself in the short run to make it easier on yourself in the long run.

CAUTION: PROGRAM ERROR

In the nineteenth century, Artemus Ward said, "It ain't the things we don't know that hurt us. It is the things we do know that ain't so." When it comes to work, truer words were never spoken. All of us have ideas, values, biases and theories about work. For purposes of simplicity, let's refer to them as "work tapes": recorded messages about work stored away in the recesses of our brain. Some of these tapes we are aware of, others dwell at the subconscious level. Nevertheless, all of them program our behavior from time to time. We acquire work tapes from sources such as parents, teachers, bosses, colleagues, experience, religion, the media and the government.

The problem is that in most situations, these tapes

are at best incomplete truths and at worst, total fantasies. Yet many of us play them automatically and practice their prescriptions with dogmatic zeal. The result is more work coupled with little or no accomplishment and accompanying frustration.

Listed below are twelve widely believed, highly mythological work tapes. This list is by no means complete or exhaustive. As you read each of them, try to think of someone you know who lives and practices or has practiced these injunctions. Is it you? If you are totally honest with yourself, you will probably see yourself in at least some of them.

Tape #1—"The More You Sweat, the More You Get"

Called by some "the buckets of sweat syndrome," this myth would have you believe that results are directly related to how hard you work. There is an abundance of proverbs floating around to reinforce the concept of equating results with sweat. "Keep your shoulder to the wheel and your nose to the grindstone"; "The harder I work, the luckier I get"; and Edison's "Genius is one percent inspiration and ninety-nine percent perspiration" —these are a few examples.

When many of us are asked the key to our success, the first thing we attribute it to is hard work. On a recent television newscast, a reporter asked a newly elected congressman what he attributed his upset victory to. "Hard work," he replied. Several months later he resigned from Congress, was convicted of illegal campaign tactics and sent to prison. Evidently, his victory took something more than hard work.

Consider too the case of Conrad Mathison, who in 1897 was president of the country's largest sugar refining company. When asked by reporters to explain his secret for success, Conrad replied:

> My success, as you call it, is due to hard work and that alone. . . . I started at the bottom. When I came west, I went to work at the old Chicago Sugar Refining Company. They put me on as a workman at $1.50 a day. . . . I was gradually promoted and was made president of the company.

What Conrad forgot to tell reporters was that he graduated from Yale, his father was president of the Chicago Sugar Refining Company and he became president only four years after starting as a workman. As Don Marquis stated, "When a man tells you he got rich through hard work, ask him *whose?*"

We hear a lot about hard work and success, but hard work and failure probably occur just as often. Some of us work hard at our jobs and get fired. Others work hard at marriages that fail. Still others study hard in school and fail to get promoted, graduate or find a job.

Sometimes hard work does make the difference between success and failure. The problem is that we tend to overstate its value and ignore other equally important criteria for success. Fortunately or unfortunately, results are seldom if ever proportional to the buckets of sweat expended. Keeping your shoulder to the wheel and your nose to the grindstone only guarantees you two things: a warped posture and a flat nose.

Tape #2—"Activity Means Productivity"

Many of us habitually confuse activity with results. This can be observed frequently on the job. Often, organizations find it hard to measure an employee's effectiveness. Consequently, activity replaces results as the yard-stick of performance. The busiest beaver is deemed the best worker and is rewarded for busy behavior rather than results.

The time clock is another great contributor to busy behavior. Many of us have nine-to-five jobs and some-times there are days when there is little or nothing to do. Still, in most cases, we are required to show up and stay the whole day, regardless of the workload. All this does is create a breeding ground for time- and energy-wasting behavior. After all, if you don't look busy, the boss may decide you aren't needed.

Ironically, we feel compelled to stay busy when we are least secure about what we should be doing. All too often we redouble our efforts after losing sight of our objectives. We try to fill a void of purpose with activity. Perhaps it's best summarized by a saying from the For-eign Legion: "When in doubt, gallop!"

The activity trap is beaten by setting goals and keeping them in focus. Failure to keep goals in focus is where most of us go astray. In the process of pursuing a goal, it's easy to get lost in a myriad of activities. The unfortunate result is that these activities become the end rather than a means to an end. It's the classic case of the tail wagging the dog. As Thoreau stated, "It's not enough to be busy . . . the question is: What are we busy about?"

Tape #3—"Efficiency Means Effectiveness"

The confusion that arises between efficiency and effectiveness was discussed earlier. The point I wish to make here is that effectiveness must precede efficiency.

How can you find the best way to achieve a goal if you don't know what the goal is?

Tape #4—"Burn the Midnight Oil"

This myth fosters the belief that results are proportionate to the amount of time spent in pursuing a goal. Career workaholics are common victims of this myth. Seen at the office at nights and on weekends, they allocate every possible moment to the job. Other things in life such as sleep, family and diversions are all placed in a distant second category of importance.

There are definite dangers involved in working long hours. First, all of us tend to get dull after expending a good amount of time on a task. We need to get away and recharge our batteries. Failure to do this hampers our enthusiasm and creativity. Second, if you acquire the long-hours habit, there is always tonight or this weekend to tackle writing that report or answering those letters. You allow Parkinson's Law into your life—work expands to fill the time available. Finally, the price that many of us pay for this type of behavior is exorbitant. Nervous breakdowns, ill health, divorce, alcoholism and premature death are all too common among those who buy the midnight oil program.

Tape #5—"The Best Way to Get the Job Done Is to Do It Yourself"

The argument for such a philosophy seems sound. You don't have to call or pay someone else to do the job and, by doing it yourself, you don't have to check up to insure that the job was satisfactorily completed. It also saves time involved in explaining to someone else what to do and how to do it.

There are times when doing it yourself is the answer. However, this is generally not the case for two reasons. First, despite your feelings of omnipotence, you have limitations. You may immerse yourself in a project only to find that you don't have the time, training or tools necessary to successfully complete it. You may even complicate the problem, making the situation worse. Anyone who has ever tackled complicated household repair and improvement projects has fallen into this trap. You run the high risk of pouring your time and energy into a bottomless pit and ending up empty-handed.

The second and more important reason for avoiding the do-it-yourself attitude is that it dilutes your effectiveness. Devoting a little of yourself to everything means committing a great deal of yourself to nothing. This leaves you unable to concentrate on those very few projects that have the highest payoff per investment of your time and energy. Why scatter your efforts like buckshot when you can concentrate them and be a big gun?

Tape #6—"The Easy Way Is the Best Way"

When that great philosopher, Linus, said, "No problem is so big or so complicated that it can't be run away from!" he was espousing the myth of taking the easy way out. Very often the easy-way tape is adopted by those who previously followed the hard-work tape. When all their hard work fails to bring the expected results, they become severely disenchanted. Instead of logically examining the situation and trying to learn from it, they simply remove one tape and plug in another.

Those who take the easy way out in life are not aware of, or choose to ignore, the investment theory of work. Unfortunately, they generally discover that path of least resistance carries a hidden price tag.

Some years ago, several students in a class I was teaching warned me to be aware of two people who were notorious for cheating on exams. When I gave the next test, I took great pains to watch the class and noticed two students behaving rather strangely and in a very suspicious manner. However, after grading the exams, I dismissed the possibility of their cheating simply because they had the two lowest grades in the class. Later, several other students came forward with adequate proof that the two *had* cheated. Their efforts to beat the system had given them only the low grades.

Those who take the easy way out take a short-term patching approach to life, leaving tomorrow up for grabs. The reality is that nothing is easy. The path of least resistance is for losers.

Tape #7—"Hard Work Is Virtuous"

One of the traditions of our society is that there is virtue and nobility in hard work. "She's a hard worker" or "He really has a lot of hustle" are considered high compliments. Richard Nixon summarized the idea when he stated, "Labor is good in itself. A man or woman at work not only makes a contribution to his fellow man, but becomes a better person by virtue of the act of working." Among values in our society, this one goes almost totally unchallenged.

To assume that any human activity carries with it one hundred percent inherent virtuousness is questionable. Hard work makes some men and breaks others. It depends on the person and the work in question. From everything I have read, I believe it would be safe to assume that Hitler was a very hard worker. If there was any nobility in his labor, I fail to see it.

Tape #8—"Work Is Not Fun"

The explanation of work in the Old Testament paints a very bleak picture. Work is regarded as a punishment for sins, and man is to spend most of his waking hours toiling away at backbreaking labor in order to survive. Thus from the Book of Genesis another pervasive value was born: Work is not to be enjoyed. Abraham Lincoln expressed the idea when he said, "My father taught me to work, but not to love it. I never did like to work, and I don't deny it. I'd rather read, tell stories, crack jokes, talk, laugh—anything but work."

Of all the programmed myths, we seem to be making our best progress toward deactivating this one. Most of us realize that the exertion of mental and physical energy is a totally natural thing. Depending on the individual and the work, work can be most enjoyable, highly unpleasant or somewhere in between. The trouble in following this tape is if you believe there is only unpleasantness in work, then that is all you will perceive. You run a high risk of shortchanging yourself of some of life's greatest satisfactions.

Tape #9—"There Is Only One Best Way"

Most of our formal education conditions us to think this way. In school we spend most of our time learning *the* solution to a problem or *the* answer to a question. All other answers are incorrect, and the person who has *the* right answer most often is the best student. After years of learing *the* right way, we carry this type of thinking into our jobs and other areas of our lives. When we learn how to do a job, it becomes *the* way to do the job. Any other approaches need not be considered. If someone else does the job differently, he must be doing it incorrectly.

When it comes to work, this type of thinking can really hurt us. Rigid, inflexible thinking keeps us from finding novel, creative, simpler and better ways to do the job.

If you ever found the one best way to do a job, how would you know you had found it? The fact is that you wouldn't. Solutions to problems are not absolute. Sweeping a floor with a broom is a good solution to the debris problem, compared to picking up dirt by hand. But what if a vacuum cleaner is available? A good rule of thumb is that there are always at least *two* good ways to do anything.

Tape #10—"More Discipline Means Less Freedom"

In the process of growing up, all of us are introduced many times to various forms of discipline. As a small child you sat at a desk arranged in a row with other desks. You weren't allowed to talk. You had to sit there unless given permission to get up. You had to come home at a certain hour and be in bed at a certain hour, perhaps when you weren't tired. After reaching adulthood, you may have been exposed to another type of discipline, that of the military services. In basic training, you were locked up, stripped of your personal identity and forced to conform to exacting standards of behavior.

With experiences such as these for reference, it's no surprise that the word "discipline" carries a negative connotation for most of us. Even though we may, in retrospect, believe it was beneficial for us, our gut-level feelings associate discipline with a loss of personal freedom. Thus we conclude that disciplining ourselves is done at the expense of limiting our freedom. We tend to think of freedom and discipline as representing two ends of a continuum—more of one means less of the other. If we step back and view freedom and discipline objectively, it becomes obvious that this is not the case. Freedom and discipline are not trade-offs. They can exist in various combinations. Consider the following four:

1. We can have low freedom and little discipline. Examples of this are high-crime areas of our cities where you can't walk the streets for fear of your life.

2. There can be high freedom and little discipline. Life among stereotypic Polynesians where the living is easy and little is accomplished would be an example of this.

3. Low freedom and high discipline can exist, and we are all most familiar with this combination. Examples are prisons, autocratic governments and dealing with the Internal Revenue Service.

4. Finally, there can be high freedom coupled with a great amount of discipline. This occurs when a person imposes self-discipline. He set his own goals, formulates a strategy and imposes order on himself. He programs himself to satisfy his own needs. He learns to make the most of his time and energy, and as a result, he works less and accomplishes more.

Tape #11—"Justice for All"

We hear a great deal about justice. Teachers, governments, lawyers, politicians and clergymen all cry out for justice. It's like motherhood. Who could be against it? Yet the fact remains that this isn't a just world. Life is not fair and never will be. There are numerous times when life deals a bad hand to us all. You did the work and someone else took all the credit. That's not fair. Someone gets the promotion because he's friendlier with the boss. That's not fair. Your boss screws up, lays the blame at your feet and you get fired. That's not fair. You work twice as hard as your neighbor and are twice as smart, but you earn half the income. That's not fair. The possibilities for injustice are infinite.

Life owes us nothing. Yet most of us behave as though we signed a contract before birth guaranteeing us a fair shake. When things don't go our way, we waste large amounts of time and energy lamenting the injustice we've been subjected to. "That's not fair!" "I got screwed!" "If it weren't for them!" "Would I do that to you?" "I get all the bad breaks."

Worse yet, many of us utilize injustice as a cop-out. The reasoning is simple. What's the use in trying if life is nothing but bad breaks? Thus, in addition to wasting time over past misfortunes, we deal ourselves a second blow by becoming immobilized. We simply give up.

The justice myth is overcome by acknowledging the reality that justice simply doesn't exist. Justice, like beauty, is in the eye of the beholder.

When fate is unkind to you, recognize the misfortune for what it is and resolve to learn something from it that will aid you in the future. Then promptly get back to the business of living, enjoying and achieving. Becoming immobile and wallowing in self-pity is not a consequence of getting the shaft. Rather, it is an irrational choice some of us make from time to time.

It's an unjust world, and there are no guarantees that you will make it if you try. However, one thing is certain: You won't make it if you don't try.

Tape #12—"We Work Best under Pressure"

Many of us like to believe that we do our best work in a pressure situation. However, a closer look generally reveals that this is a type of wishful thinking used by those trying to justify procrastination. The rationalization goes something like this: "Because I work better when the pressure is really on, I'll wait until the last minute. This will really get me psyched up. Then I'll turn on the after-burners, give it all I've got and do a superior job." It's a superb and common form of self-delusion.

Few if any of us ever do our best work under pressure, despite what we would like to believe. Before subjecting yourself to a pressure situation in the future, you should consider the following potential consequences.

First, if you are forced to work at an accelerated pace, you increase the odds of making mistakes. If you do make a crucial mistake, you may not have time to correct it.

Second, pressure situations make you extremely vulnerable to Murphy's Law:

Nothing is as easy as it looks.

33

Everything takes longer than you expect.
And if anything can go wrong, it will—
At the worst possible moment!

Something may come up that's extremely urgent and rob you of those few precious moments you allocated to doing the job. You wait until the night before to write that important report for the boss, and the roof starts to leak, or your spouse gets sick, or the typewriter breaks. As a result you end up not doing the job or botching it up so badly that you have to start all over. If you didn't have time to do it right the first time, where are you going to find the time to do it again?

Third, assuming all went well and you did get a lot done in a little time, it only means you know how to be effective but don't choose to unless you are under pressure. You are cheating yourself by failing to become more of what you are capable of. In the words of Linus, "There's no heavier burden than a great potential!"

Finally, if you don't get the job done and you could have done it by starting earlier, you will probably suffer a loss of confidence and self-esteem. Who needs that?

Turn Off Those Tapes

When you allow irrational beliefs such as the foregoing to govern your behavior, your time and energy are channeled into unproductive efforts. Therefore, a giant step toward working smart is to track down any irrational beliefs about work you may be clinging to, get them out in the open and see them for what they are. Irrational thoughts must be consciously exposed before you can work on banishing them from your life.

Start replacing those old ideas that don't work with

34

ones that do. Turn off those old worn-out tapes and replace them with viable programs designed to increase your awareness, flexibility and productivity. It's not easy. It involves recognition, motivation and change. But is it ever worth it!

CHAPTER 2

It's Your Life—
Goals of the Game

*"If you really know what things you
want out of life, it's amazing how
opportunities will come to enable you
to carry them out."*

—John M. Goddard

Human beings are naturally goal-seeking creatures. When we have no goals, we live an aimless and purposeless life. The next time someone tells you they feel life is not worthwhile or that they are bored, take a closer look. What they are really saying is that they have no worthwhile problems to solve, obstacles to conquer or goals to achieve.

Developing a successful plan for effectiveness begins with goal setting. You can make a very good case that goals and the sense of purpose that accompanies them are necessary for survival. Actuaries report high incidences of poor health and death shortly after the mandatory retirement age. After forty to fifty years in a job or career, it is understandable that someone feels stripped of his sense of direction and value when retirement is thrust upon him. Many of us reach retirement totally unprepared, with no other goals to pursue, and as a result we rust out rather than wear out.

Contrast the retirement syndrome to the fact that many creative people such as artists and composers often enjoy much greater than average longevity. Many live well into their eighties and nineties, and their final years are often the most productive. Unlike most of us, they die with their boots on. Am I saying that artists tend to live longer because they are more creative? That's not the point at all. Rather, I believe the artists' longevity is attributable to an unending and uninterrupted sense of purpose and direction. To these people there is always another symphony to compose or canvas to fill.

We can't all be artists, but we all need and can have goals. Of course, we all have some goals. However, the overwhelming majority of them are vague and poorly conceived. Few of us ever undertake the task of setting some definite goals for our life. Doing this would greatly increase the odds of working less and accomplishing more. Until we decide what we want, we aren't very likely to get it. In the meantime, we flounder around working more and accomplishing less by frittering away our time and energy aimlessly.

GUIDELINES FOR SETTING GOALS

Most of us recognize the importance of goals. However, when it comes to the task of setting specific goals, we back off or procrastinate. We feel uneasy about it. Planning our life seems like such an onerous task that most of us simply throw up our hands and say, in effect, "I just don't know where to begin."

Here is a program that will provide the structure you

need to get you started on your way to meaningful goal setting. If you follow these instructions and guidelines, the task of goal setting will become far less burdensome. In fact, you will probably enjoy it.

An Exercise in Self-Discovery

It makes little sense to decide what you want out of life until you have a good idea of who you are. This is why the following self-discovery exercise precedes goal setting. Once you have established a sense of who you are you will be in a better position to set meaningful goals.

Take ten index cards. On one side of each card write the following incomplete statement: My name is (your name) and I am a(n) _____. Now take about ten minutes and complete each statement differently. Work rapidly, as the objective of this exercise is to discover your true feelings about yourself. Don't censor any answers that come to your mind. Write them down. Answers such as gambler, alcoholic, or ping-pong fiend are no less valid than answers like human being, parent, student, wife, homeowner or sports fan.

You may find you need more than ten cards. That's fine. Use as many as you need. Some people find it difficult to come up with ten answers. This is generally due to censoring their thoughts. If you encounter this problem, perform this exercise where you will be alone and undisturbed. Most of all, remember that there are no right or wrong answers. That key is spontaneity.

When you have completed all ten statements, read them over, arrange them in order of importance and number them. Then turn over the first card and complete the following statement: "This 'I am' is first because _____." Do the same for the remaining cards, in order.

39

Now take a moment to look over your self-discovery cards and reflect on them. Imagine that these cards were written by someone else, and write the answers to the following questions:

1. What do these cards tell you about this person?
2. What things are most important to him?
3. What types of things would this person enjoy doing with his life that you aren't doing?
4. How would you recommend that this person spend his life if he had only six months to live?

Keep the self-discovery cards and the answers to the above questions nearby. You will want to refer to them as you formulate your goals.

Setting Up Your Goals

In trying to decide what you want out of life it helps to break down your life into manageable units. In order to do that, try this exercise. Take six more index cards or sheets of paper and label each with one of the following headings: career goals, personal relationship goals, recreational goals, personal growth goals, material goals and prestige goals. Next, pick up each card and write down some goals that you think you would like to achieve. As in the first exercise, work rapidly and don't censor your impulses. If you think you would like to do it, it's a potential goal.

Be sure your goals are your own! I cannot emphasize this point too strongly. It's your life. Take charge of it and do what's meaningful to you. If there is any one concept in this book that supersedes that importance of having goals, it is that your goals must be set by you and not someone else.

Unfortunately, most of us allow our goals to be set by employers, parents, spouses, children, the government or whatever. It's far more difficult to set your own goals and be your own person when there exists a myriad of forces persuading you to do otherwise.

Setting your own goals and striving to achieve them is a major step toward personal freedom and a meaningful life. This doesn't preclude your doing what others want you to do or soliciting suggestions from others about what your goals should be. In fact, talking and listening to friends or relatives who know you well may trigger some meaningful goals you wouldn't have thought of alone. But the final decision on your goals must be yours. As Christopher Morley stated, "There is only one success —to be able to spend your life in your own way."

At this point you may be thinking that all this rhetoric about setting your own goals is interesting but somewhat unrealistic. When I discuss the importance of self-set goals in seminars a common response is "Sure, I'd like to open my own business, or go back to school, or live somewhere else, or change careers, but I have to face reality." Then I hear a number of excuses such as I'm too old, my spouse would leave me, my parents are getting old, I have to think about my children and so on. Actually, this kind of reasoning is little more than a fear of failure and an attempt to cling to security in a world where there is none.

My good friend Dennis Had is a classic example of the value of personal goal setting. In 1974, Denny was completing his sixth year as a stockbroker and by society's standards he was a portrait of middle-class American success. He had a happy marriage, three thriving children, a home, two cars and an ulcer. Though financially

41

successful as a stockbroker, the nature of the work didn't fit Denny's temperament. He longed for something more tangible and felt frustrated by the inability to control his own destiny.

Denny overcame his frustrations by waking up to the fact that only he and divine providence can control his destiny. An avid amateur radio operator since childhood, Denny decided to form the Dentron Radio Company and manufacture and sell equipment for ham radio operators.

In April 1974, Denny quit his job, sold the family cars to acquire capital, borrowed to the hilt on credit cards and began making amateur radio equipment in his basement. Dentron was born. Many of Denny's friends and relatives watched with sorrow and dismay, feeling certain that he had lost his mind.

On August 28, 1974, Dentron Radio recorded its first sale. In April 1975, Dentron moved from Denny's basement to the Dentron plant in Twinsburg, Ohio. By the end of 1975 Dentron had grossed over $1 million in sales.

Today, Denny Had finds himself the owner and president of a growing multi-million dollar manufacturing and marketing operation which sells products to amateur radio enthusiasts and governments throughout the world. Boundless energy and enthusiasm for life characterize the Denny Had of today. He is a living testament to James Barrie's statement: "Nothing is really work unless you would rather be doing something else."

The Denny Had method for achieving goals is simple. "Once you decide on what you want, put on the blinders and move full speed ahead. Don't listen to anyone else because they will only tell you why something can't be done," says Denny. Not too surprisingly, his ulcer vanished years ago.

Listed below are several examples of each of the types of goals in this exercise. I don't mean to imply that any of these should or should not be your goals. They are here merely for the purpose of illustration. If you think of a goal that falls into more than one category, write it down on each appropriate card. A goal appearing several times is usually a good one because it indicates a wide range of potential satisfaction to you.

Career Goals
- Become president of the company by age forty.
- Get promoted this year.
- Find another career more in line with my tastes and aptitudes.
- Open my own restaurant.
- Get transferred to the home office.
- Become top salesman in my district.
- Get my boss's job.
- Get a job with my company's competitor.
- Quit work and become a college professor.
- Pass the CPA examination.

Personal Relationship Goals
- Devote two hours eacy day to getting to know my children better.
- Take at least one escape weekend every three months with my spouse.
- Try to meet at least one new person each day.
- Convert a former adversary to a friend.

- Fall in love.
- Get married.
- Get a divorce.
- Cultivate one new, close friendship each month.
- Learn to remember names.
- Evict my mother-in-law.

Recreational Goals
- Find a better way to loaf each day.
- Go on a safari.
- Attend an orgy.
- Get an amateur radio license and talk to people around the world.
- Buy a boat.
- Write a novel.
- Take a trip around the world.
- Raise Great Danes.
- Sleep late on Saturdays.
- Watch the sunset.

Personal Growth Goals
- Learn one new word each day.
- Take a speed-reading course.
- Learn to make better use of my time and energy.
- Attend a lecture on something I know little or nothing about each month.
- Learn to control my temper.
- Take up conversational French.
- Go away to college.
- Join the Marines.
- Spend a night on skid row or in jail.
- Volunteer for charity work.

Material Goals
- Be financially independent in five years.
- Buy a house this year.
- Get a sports car.
- Buy the best in quadraphonic stereo.
- Buy a motorcycle.
- Buy a yacht and live on it.
- Acquire rental property.
- Add another bathroom to the house.
- Earn enough money to pay off the mortgage.

Social Goals
- Join the country club.
- Make the dean's list.
- Graduate with honors.
- Run for political office.
- Wear expensive clothes.
- Move to an impressive neighborhood.
- Throw formal dinner parties for important people.
- Be captain of the football team.
- Be chosen employee of the month.
- Appear on radio or television as an expert.

Be sure to refer back to your self-discovery cards as you begin to write down your goals. They will be a great help in pointing the way toward which goals will be most meaningful. If, for example, one of your self-discovery cards says "I am a father," logical goals might be to set aside more time each week for getting better acquainted with your children or adding a family recreation room to your house. If one of your cards says "golfer," saving for a new set of clubs or resolving to lower your score by five strokes by the end of the year would be potential goals. The idea is to use the self-discovery cards as a guide to which things in life are most meaningful to you.

The reason for putting goals in writing is twofold. First, writing goals helps you identify more clearly what you want. Most of us never write down our goals. We are simply content to think about them. However, thoughts are fleeting and if our goals are merely thoughts, we run a high risk of having little more than daydreams. Written goals are less likely to be forgotten or lost in the shuffle of daily routines.

Writing down goals also increases your personal commitment to them. As you take the time to think about your life and what you want out of it, you are applying the investment theory of work to planning. This is an investment of your time which has one of the highest potential payoffs. Making the effort to write down goals means giving more of yourself to a goal than merely thinking about it. And the degree of commitment you have to a goal is the single most important factor in achieving it.

When you have completed this exercise, you have the first rough draft of your goals Setting goals is much like writing an essay or a report. You begin with getting a few ideas down on paper and then set about the task of refining, polishing and shaping them into a cohesive entity. The following guidelines are designed to aid you in transforming your ideas about what you would like to do into a cohesive plan for getting the most from your life.

Set Challenging but Attainable Goals

Some years ago an experiment in achievement motivation was undertaken in a downtown office building.

About fifteen people were invited to participate in a ring-toss game. A spike was placed at one end of the room and each player was given several rope rings to pitch onto the spike. Each player was allowed to stand as far from the spike as he wished when throwing his rings. Those players who stood close to the spike hit the target with ease and quickly lost interest. Some players stood far away, failed to make any ringers and quickly became discouraged. However, a few players stood far enough away to make the game challenging but close enough for success to be attainable. The experimenters interpreted this as a sign that these people had a high degree of achievement motivation. High achievers are usually hooked on getting satisfaction by continually setting challenging but attainable goals.

Achievement motivation experts such as David McClelland believe that the need to achieve can be learned. One major step is to set a goal that you believe you can achieve but also causes you to stretch your abilities.

As you search through your goals cards, seek out those goals that are attainable and challenging. Unattainable goals aren't goals—they are fantasies. What is an attainable goal is a decision that only you can make. If you think you can do it and it seems right, then it's attainable and I urge you to pursue it.

Make Your Goals as Specific and Measureable as Possible

The more specific you make your goals, the more direction they will provide for you. For example, if your goal is to buy a house, start trying to pin down what

47

you have in mind. What size house? How many stories? How many bedrooms? Brick or frame? What size lot? Located where? What price range? And so on. If your goal is to be financially independent, sit down with a pencil and paper and decide how much money you will have to acquire. The amount of money necessary for financial independence is a very personal decision. For some $100,000 is plenty, whereas for others $1 million isn't enough.

Several years ago, setting a specific goal saved me a great deal of time and effort. My goal was to buy a house. I wrote down many details about the type of house I was looking for and began to read the want ads. Ten days later, I answered an advertisement for a house in the neighborhood I wanted to live in. The house fit every detail I had listed except one: The price was twenty percent less than I had expected to pay. I purchased the house and have been living in it happily ever since. It was the first house I bothered to look at, and I found it without the aid of a realtor. Of course I was lucky. But remember that luck is opportunity meeting preparation. Specifying clearly what you want will save you a great deal of time.

Not all goals are as easy to measure as income or housing specifications. Goals such as being a good parent or a responsible citizen cannot be quantified. In these cases, you can construct a rating scale from one to ten with one representing the poorest and ten representing the ultimate. Then you can estimate where on the scale you think you are now and decide where you would like to be.

If you don't feel a rating scale is appropriate you can always try verbally describing what you want as vividly as you can. For example, if your goal is to improve your appearance, answer questions such as what can I do to my hair, skin, teeth, eyes, weight and dress in order to improve my appearance. This type of describing gives you much more direction than simply saying "I want to look better."

If you find that you cannot quantify it, measure it, rate it or describe it, you probably can forget it as a goal.

Check Your Goals for Compatibility

In the process of setting your goals it is possible to set two or more goals where the attainment of one prevents the attainment of the other(s). You want to be a sales manager but don't want to give up the personal freedom you have as a sales representative. You want to be the best in your profession (which frequently requires working long hours and weekends) but you want to spend more time with your family. You want to vacation abroad this year but the house needs a new roof and you can't afford both. These are common examples of incompatible goals.

Or you may pour you time and energy into several projects only to find out you can't complete them all. Goal incompatibility can lead to uncertainty and indecision about which goals to pursue. Often the result is that you pursue no goals at all. Examine your goals for incompatibility at the outset. It may save you a great deal of time and frustration.

Consider Your Goals Flexible

Many of us shy away from writing goals because we feel that putting goals on paper is tantamount to carving them in stone for the ages. This is an idea that needs to be dispelled here and now. As a viable, growing person your needs and values will be forever evolving. Consequently you will have to reevaluate and often modify, discard or replace some of your goals. If you don't do this to some degree, then you aren't giving much thought to where you are going, or you may be thinking of goals as rigid and inflexible.

A good plan is like a comfortable shoe. It serves its purpose and flexes to accommodate the needs of the user. Keep this in mind when setting and evaluating your goals.

Setting Target Dates

A good rule to impose on yourself in this: A goal doesn't become a goal until you have a deadline for accomplishment. Target dates for goal achievement are another step in increasing your motivation and commitment. When you have a major goal to accomplish, break it down into subgoals and put deadlines on them. As you meet subgoal target dates you will feel the satisfaction and pride that comes with meaningful progress. This in turn will create even greater momentum toward achieving the major goals. Target dates, like goals, should be realistic.

To help you set realistic target dates, consider each goal from a relative time perspective. For purposes of simplicity, let's divide our goals into three time categories:

Lifetime Goals—Results that you wish to accomplish or things you want to experience in your lifetime. Often, though not necessarily, these goals are long-range and take more than one year to accomplish.

Intermediate Goals—Goals you wish to accomplish in less than one year.

Daily Goals—Seeing that you make the most of each day.

All of these goals must be considered in light of each other. The daily goals should contribute to the achievement of intermediate goals. Likewise, intermediate goals should be set to contribute to lifetime goals. The objective is to coordinate your use of time and energy for maximum effectiveness. The concept of coordinating a hierarchy of goals called goal congruency. As you place your goals in a time perspective you may want to modify, add to or reject some of them in the interest of goal congruency. Most of us don't do this. When we fail to relate our todays to our tomorrows, we find ourselves starting from scratch each day. We are left with the grim realization that our wheels are spinning but we aren't going anywhere. Let's not have this happen to you.

Take a sheet of paper and label it Lifetime Goals. Based on what you have written, you should have little trouble in coming up with a number of goals. Many of them will be very broad. That's okay. The purpose of lifetime goals is to provide a general direction for your life. To believe you can plan your entire lifetime in specific detail is unrealistic. Your intermediate goals will be more specific and daily goals should be the most specific of all.

You will want to update your lifetime goals list periodically. As you mature you may expect goals to be added and deleted from your list. As was pointed out earlier, good planning is flexible.

Setting Intermediate Goals—Project Planning

Most of us think of intermediate goals as projects —things we would like to accomplish in the foreseeable future, usually less than one year. Projects can bridge the gap between lifetime goals and daily activities.

The following is a project-planning exercise. Take several sheets of paper and answer the following questions and statements:

1. State clearly and specifically a goal you would like to achieve in the next six months.

2. Why do you want to achieve this goal?

3. If you succeed, what will it do for you?

4. How much do you want to achieve this goal?

5. How will achieving this goal contribute to the attainment of your lifetime goals?

6. What price will you have to pay to achieve this goal? Are you willing to pay it?

7. Estimate your chances of achieving this goal.

8. What will happen if you fail?

9. List the major subgoals involved in achieving this goal and assign a target date to each.

10. What obstacles stand between you and successful completion of your project? How will you overcome them?

11. What can you do today that will start you on the path to achieving this goal?

Which brings us to:

Setting Daily Goals—the To-Do List

Those of you who habitually set daily goals know the value of the daily to-do list. A well-known story about the efficacy of a to-do list concerns Charles Schwab when he was president of Bethlehem Steel. He called in Ivy Lee, a consultant, and said, "Show me a way to get more things done with my time, and I'll pay you any fee within reason."

"Fine," Lee replied. "I'll give you something in twenty minutes that will step up your output at least fifty percent."

With that, Lee handed Schwab a blank piece of paper and said, "Write down the six most important tasks that you have to do tomorrow and number them in order of their importance. Now put this paper in your pocket and the first thing tomorrow morning look at item one and start working on it until you finish it. Then do item two, and so on. Do this until quitting time and don't be concerned if you have finished only one or two. You'll be working on the most important ones first anyway. If you can't finish them all by this method, you couldn't have by any other method either; and without some system you'd probably not even have decided which was the most important."

Then Lee said, "try this system every working day. After you've convinced yourself of the value of the system, have your men try it. Try it as long as you wish and then send me a check for what you think it's worth."

Several weeks later Schwab sent Lee a check for $25,000 with a note proclaiming the advice the most profitable he had ever followed. This concept helped Charles Schwab earn $100 million and turn Bethelehem Steel into the biggest independent steel producer in the world.

You may think Charles Schwab was foolish to pay $25,000 for such a simple idea. However, Schwab thought of that consulting fee as one of his best investments.

"Sure it was a simple idea," Schwab said. "But what ideas are not basically simple? For the first time, my entire team and myself are getting first things done first."

Start each day by making a daily to-do list. Make this practice as habitual as brushing your teeth or having that morning cup of coffee. Write down all the things you want to accomplish that day and rank them in order of importance. The small amount of time and effort you invest in this practice will repay you many times over. Make sure your to-do list is on one sheet of paper rather than several sheets. Also, make the list on a pad or piece of paper small enough to carry in your pocket or purse. It should go where you go. If you're ever tempted to keep your to-do list in your head, remember what Ziggy said: "I made a mental note to remember something very important I had to do today . . . but I lost the note."

SETTING PRIORITIES—THE 80/20 RULE

If you carried out the exercises on goal setting previously described, you probably had little trouble in coming up with many goals. In fact, you probably have enough goals to last you several lifetimes. However, the simple fact is that you have only one life. You are now faced with the prospect of setting priorities—deciding which goals are most important to your overall happiness and fulfillment. Setting priorities is simply a matter of putting first things first.

The simplest system for setting priorities is to rank goals in order of importance as Charles Schwab did on his to-do list. Other people, such as time-management

consultant Alan Lakein, use the A, B, C method. Goals
are first put into three categories:

(A) Must do

(B) Should do

(C) Nice to do

Then each set of goals is ranked in order. Thus your
top-priority item is labeled A-1. The idea is to start with
A's and only do C's if you complete all the A's and
B's.

It makes little difference which type of priority system you use as long as it works for you. I find the simple
numbering system works for me. Others enjoy being creative and color-code their lists. Top-priority items are
underlined in red, medium-priority in blue and so on.

The 80/20 rule, or Pareto principle (named after
Vilfredo Pareto, a nineteenth-century Italian economist),
explains why setting priorities is so important in securing
effectiveness. This rule states that eighty percent of the
value of a group of items is generally concentrated in only
twenty percent of the items. It's an interesting concept,
and there are plenty of examples in life that tend to
validate the 80/20 rule. Eighty percent of the dollar value
of an inventory is often found in twenty percent of the
items. Eighty percent of all telephone calls comes from
twenty percent of the callers. Eighty percent of the meals
ordered in a restaurant come from twenty percent of the
items on the menu. Eighty percent of all television viewing
is spent watching twenty percent of all programs. If you
keep the 80/20 rule in mind you will find it appearing in
many different places.

However, our use of the 80/20 rule applies to goals.
Simply put, it means you can be eighty percent effective

by achieving twenty percent of your goals. If you have a daily to-do list of ten items, this means you can generally expect to be eighty percent effective by successfully completing only the two most important items on your list! How's that for good news? The main idea is that to be effective you must concentrate on the most important items first.

2

Launching Yourself

CHAPTER 3

Getting Organized

*"Organizing is what you do before you do
something, so that when you do it,
it's not all mixed up."*

—*Christopher Robin*
in *A. A. Milne's* Winnie the Pooh

In one of his films, W. C. Fields plays an executive whose desk top is a morass of clutter. In one scene he returns to his desk to find that an efficiency expert has organized, rearranged and streamlined it. The desk top is now a picture of neatness and efficiency, but Fields is frustrated. He can't find anything! So he vigorously throws the neat stacks of paper up in the air, tossing them in the way a gourmet would a salad. Then he backs off, surveys the desk top with satisfaction, deftly reaches into the pileup and pulls out the desired document.

To fully appreciate the satire of that scene we should place it in historical perspective. At the time Fields was in his glory, efficiency exerts were preaching the gospel of organization. One of the cardinal sins of inefficiency was to have a desk that had anything on top of it other than the immediate work at hand. A clear desk was heralded as the badge of efficiency and productivity.

Today we are less sure of this. Certainly a life of organization is usually a great deal more effective than one of chaos. Most of us could enhance our effectiveness with more organization. However, hard and fast rules are not the order of the day when it comes to organizing. This is what W. C. Fields was trying to tell us in the film. We all must organize to suit our own personality and the task at hand.

As you plan your life, resist the temptation of becoming overly organized—it's an effectiveness killer. I had a friend in college who flunked out after one semester. The main reason was that he spent all of his study time reading various books on how to study and never got around to studying. The same problem can arise as you try to work smarter. Remember, these ideas are merely means to an end and that end is to increase your lifetime effectiveness. Running around with a stopwatch and keeping a totally clear desk isn't going to accomplish what you want in life.

Nevertheless, there are some good guidelines for organizing your life and your thoughts, and those are discussed in this chapter. If you practice these guidelines as guidelines rather than as hard and fast rules, you will find they will aid you in getting the most from your time and effort. With that thought in mind, let's look at a few of them.

GET THE PROPER TOOLS TO DO THE JOB

Thomas Carlyle once remarked, "Man is a tool-using animal ... without tools he is nothing, with tools he is all." Those are words worth remembering. How many times have you labored at an unsuccessful activity only to find out that having a particular tool could have saved you a great deal of time, energy and frustration? This type of experience is usually most apparent to us when we are trying to repair the family car or something around the house. This is because we tend to think of tools as tangible instruments, as many of them are. However, to make the most of this guideline we have to use the word "tool" in a much broader context.

A tool is anything you use to help you achieve your goals. No matter what your goals or what activities you pursue, all of them involve tools. If you are an accountant your tools include the obvious pencils, papers and calculators as well as your CPA certificate and your practical knowledge. If you work in an office, the office itself with its desk, chair and floor space is a tool.

Other examples of less obvious tools are automobiles, statistical tables, newspapers, foreign languages and interviewing techniques. The list is endless.

Before setting out to perform a task or achieve a goal stop and ask yourself, "What are the necessary tools to complete the task successfully, and do I have them?" If you don't have the proper tools, first consider getting someone else to do the job. Your time, energy and expenses may be greatly reduced by employing someone else. However, if it's something only you can do, make an effort to first equip yourself with the best tools available. The difference between wise men and fools is often found in their choice of tools.

ORGANIZE YOUR WORKSPACE

Consider the environment in which you will be performing the task. Organizing your workspace is largely a personal matter that depends on your own tastes and the job to be done. However, there are several basic factors to keep in mind:

1. Location. If you are fortunate enough to choose your workspace, choose one that is conducive to performing the task. If the job requires concentration, look for a quiet, private place. On the other hand, if you are opening your own business, choose a well-traveled location where potential customers have easy access to your establishment.

2. Space. After you have chosen the proper work location, measure how much space you have to work with. Most of us usually find we have less than we want. It helps to know what space is available before furnishing it with the necessary tools.

3. Easy access to the tools you use frequently. It helps here to make a list of the tools you use and rank them in order of how often you use them. Then you will have a guide to arranging them for easiest access.

Refrain from cluttering your workspace with nonessential items. The moosehead you had mounted after your last hunting trip to Canada may well be a sight worth seeing, but if it distracts you, you should place it somewhere else. Besides, it may occupy space where a more useful tool such as a memo board could be put.

4. Comfort. Some people don't believe that workspaces should be designed for comfort. They are generally people who play the hard-work tape or the work-is-inher-

ently-unpleasant tape The fact is that discomfort is a distraction that serves only to hinder productivity. Why make things more difficult than they have to be? Life is already filled with a more than ample supply of discomforts, distractions and frustrations.

A comfortable workspace generally has the proper seating, ventilation and lighting. If you work sitting down for long periods, choose a firm, comfortable chair that gives good back support. Try to find one comfortable enough that you won't have to get up every ten minutes, but not so comfortable that you will fall asleep in it. To avoid eyestrain use indirect, uniform lighting.

Adequate ventilation will help prevent unnecessary fatigue from stuffiness in the work environment. Which temperature range you work best in is a personal matter. However, be sure to locate your place in the workspace out of a draft.

MASTER THE ART OF DESKMANSHIP

A great many of us perform some or all of our work at a desk. As I mentioned earlier, a desk is a tool—and it is one of the most abused and misused of tools. So before delving into the application of this tool and how to get the most from it, we ought to consider what a desk is not.

Specifically, a desk is *not:*

1. A place to conduct a paper drive. Judging from the many cluttered desk tops I've seen, I'm convinced that paper recyclers would fare better if they raided desk tops in office buildings rather than collecting old newspapers from the local shopping center.

2. A storage depot for food, clothing, umbrellas and other nonjob sundries. I once moved into an office only to find I was sharing a desk with a colony of ants. It seems that my predecessor had willed me a large open bag of candy in the top right-hand drawer, but the clever little devils had beaten me to it.

3. A place to stack items you want to remember. A German executive once remarked to Alec Mackenzie that desk tops get stacked because we put things there we don't want to forget. The problem is that it works. Every time we look up, we see all these things we don't want to forget and our mind wanders, breaking our train of thought. With time, the stacks grow higher and we forget what's in each one. So we waste large amounts of time retrieving lost items and thinking about all those things we don't want to forget. Merrill Douglass, a time-management consultant, tells of keeping a close time log on one executive who had a stacked desk. The log revealed that he spent two-and-a-half hours per day looking for information on the top of his desk!

4. A status symbol or place to display awards, trophies and the like. This mistaken use of desks causes us only to make desks larger than they have to be. With more surface area we have more room for clutter and somehow more clutter magically appears to fill up any available space.

Now that we have discussed what a desk is not, let's look at what a desk is. It's a tool that expedites the receiving and processing of information and should be utilized with those objectives in mind.

You may have a desk and not need one. Lawrence

Appley, former president of the American Management Association, remarked that most desks only bury decisions. Some executives have thrown out their desks and declared their effectiveness has increased. They have replaced the standard office desk and chair with a lounge chair, clipboard, small writing table on casters, and file cabinets. Advocates of the deskless office report an improvement in face-to-face communication and an atmosphere of greater freedom. They no longer feel chained to a desk. Consider the possibility that you may not need a desk and, if you can get rid of it, try working without it and see what happens.

How to Reorganize Your Desk for Effectiveness

Assuming you do need your desk, you may want to embark on a reorganization project. If you decide to reorganize your desk, block out several hours in your schedule when you won't be interrupted. Desk reorganization is a good Saturday morning project and can be accomplished by the following procedure:

1. Get a large trash can.

2. Take everything off the top of the desk and empty all drawers. Discard every item that is no longer of any use.

3. Make a list of all the remaining items that were in or on your desk and rank them in order of importance. When you consider each item ask yourself "What's the worst thing that will happen if I throw this away?" If the answer isn't very bad, throw away the item and leave it off the list.

4. Critically view all the nondiscarded items and put only the most essential ones in your desk. Articles that

you don't need immediate access to should be stored somewhere else, such as in a file cabinet or bookcase.

5. Make a filing system in the deep drawers, with files well labeled and organized for quick and easy access. Periodically review all of your desk files and keep only the current essential ones in your desk. Over ninety percent of all files over one year old are never referred to.

6. To use the input-output principle for processing information, get two large stacking file baskets—one to store incoming work and one for storing work you have processed and are ready to send on. Pending items of low priority or needing later attention may be filed in the desk drawer, as long as the drawers are regularly monitored.

Guidelines for Working at a Desk

If you have gone to the trouble of reorganizing your desk, you have taken a giant step toward making your desk a more effective tool. Some find it helpful to repeat desk reorganization every six months. The following guidelines are designed to increase your desk-work effectiveness by reducing the amount of clutter.

1. Have only one project at a time on top of your desk—it should be your top priority for the moment.

2. Keep items off your desk until you are ready for them. Store them in file cabinets or drawers, but get them out of sight.

3. Don't allow yourself to be sidetracked by other tasks because they are easier or more appealing. You should work on the top-priority item and keep at it until it is completed.

4. When you complete a task, put it in the out basket and send it on its way. Then check your priorities and move on to the next item.

5. If you have one, a secretary can help by keeping your desk clear and seeing that the day's top-priority item is waiting on your desk at the beginning of each day.

As I pointed out earlier, these are merely guidelines and they may not be suitable for you. Making a fetish out of a clean desk isn't going to get the job done, and for some it becomes just another detractor from effectively doing the job. Choose a style suitable for you and the work to be done, but be honest with yourself. Few of us do our best work with a heavily cluttered and disorganized desk.

IMPROVE YOUR ABILITY TO CONCENTRATE

Concentration in any form is an amazing phenomenon. As a six-year-old, I was spellbound when one of my friends ignited a piece of paper by focusing the sun's rays on the paper through a magnifying glass. Our own time and energy are much like the sun's rays. To the degree that we concentrate our efforts we will succeed in getting what we want out of life. The ability to concentrate has enabled many men of modest capabilities to reach heights of success that have often eluded geniuses.

In a sense, this entire book is aimed toward helping you improve your ability to concentrate. Many of the ideas previously discussed, such as setting goals and priorities and getting the proper tools and work environment, will aid you in successfully concentrating. There are several other organizational guidelines aimed at improving your concentration.

Think with a Pencil in Your Hand

If you tried the goal-setting exercises in Chapter 2, you already have a good idea of the value of thinking on paper. When you write down your ideas you automatically focus your full attention on them. Few if any of us can write one thought and think another at the same time. Thus a pencil and paper make excellent concentration tools.

Whenever you need to concentrate, make it a habit to think with a pencil in your hand. As ideas come to you, jot them down. As you write down ideas, you will automatically be thinking them through and clarifying them in your mind. Soon you will have a list of thoughts to consider. You will be much more likely to see which ideas are irrational, erroneous or in conflict with each other if you can view them all at once.

Reserve Your Work Place Exclusively for Work

We are all creatures of habit, and most of our behavior involves little or no thought. We learn to associate certain behavior with a given environment. If we don't take pains to develop good habits in the work environment, all sorts of unproductive ones can develop and rob us of our time and energy.

One way to improve your ability to concentrate is to reserve your work place only for working. For example, if you work behind a desk in an office, don't do anything at your desk unrelated to work. If a visitor drops in, get up and move away from the desk. If you allow yourself to socialize behind the desk you will come to associate that location as more than a work location. When you take a break, move away from where you work. Sit in another chair or go to another room. If you develop the habit of choosing a certain spot to work, you will find yourself getting down to business much more rapidly and automatically when it's time to work.

Slow Down and Stop Constructively

One of the keys to the art of staying with a task is in knowing how and when to back off. Blind perseverance is for fools. It involves working harder rather than smarter.

When you find yourself mentally blocked from solving problems, make a tactical retreat from your work. Pushing ahead will only lead to confusion and frustration. Perhaps you need to get more input about the task or need more time to digest and integrate information.

When you have to quit working, there are several things you can do to make your work more enjoyable and productive when you start back:

1. Try to end your work on a high note. If you quit at a point of satisfaction, you will tend to think of the work as gratifying and be more eager to return to it.

2. Try to stop at a point of accomplishment.

3. If you quit at a point where you are stalled, write down the problem and try to clarify what's blocking your progress.

4. Have a logical starting point at which to resume. This will reduce your start-up time when you return to the task.

IMPROVE YOUR FOLLOW-THROUGH

Knowing when to stop is a good tactical maneuver, but it doesn't get the job done. Somewhere along the line you must tackle the task and follow through to completion. Here are some ideas that you will find helpful in successfully finishing what you start. Some of them have been, or will be, discussed in greater detail elsewhere.

1. Get interested in your work. Interest and motivation go together like Siamese twins. Get more information. The more you know about something, the greater the odds you will become absorbed in it.

2. Try to imagine the satisfaction that will come from seeing the task achieved. Think of how much better you'll look after you've shed those twenty pounds or how much better you'll feel when you quit smoking. Think of the better job you will have and the happier life you'll lead when you finally get that degree or that promotion. As I write this book I imagine myself walking past a bookstore and seeing the book in the window. I imagine people telling me how this book helped them to lead happier lives. I imagine all the things I'll be able to do with the royalty checks. You know what? I'm really getting excited! Let's move on to the next idea so I can finish the book.

3. Challenge yourself with deadlines for completion.

4. Try to shield yourself from interruptions and distractions.

5. Take part in a joint effort with someone else who is dependable. When you make a commitment to do something with someone else, you are more likely to do the job than if you tackle it alone. When I was in graduate school we would study in groups or pairs to reinforce our

commitment to learn. We called it "cooperate and graduate." The important thing is that each person be dependable. If both parties are committed, each can set the pace for the other.

IMPROVE YOUR MEMORY

One of our greatest time- and energy-saving tools is our memory. Without a memory all of our learning would be useless. We would have to respond to every situation as if we had never experienced it. We use our memories to learn to walk, talk, absorb facts, solve problems, drive cars, read and do numerous other things. The uses and capacity of the human memory are a miracle. You can store more bits of information in your two-pound brain than in today's most advanced computers.

Unfortunately, storing information is one thing and retrieving it is another. This is where the computer is our superior. However, most of us can improve our ability to store and retrieve information if we understand how our memory works and apply some simple concepts of memory improvement.

Your memory is not a thing, it's a test of skills. It can't be seen, felt, examined or weighed. Memory skills are generally divided into three stages:

(1) Remembering—Leaving the information to be stored.

(2) Recording—Storing the material in the brain until needed.

(3) Retrieving—Getting the material out when needed. This final stage is the cause of our greatest problems. How many times have you said to yourself, "It's on the tip of my tongue?"

We can do little or nothing to improve our retrieval

ability per se. However, our ability to retrieve is somewhat dependent on how we record information, and we can improve our memory by modifying our methods of recording. Briefly, here are some guidelines to aid you in making the most of your memory:

1. Commit things to memory when you are rested. If you try to memorize when you are fatigued, you will most likely find it frustrating.

2. Break down lists into smaller, manageable units and subcategories before trying to memorize them. If you have to learn the capital cities of twenty nations, break them up into five groups of four, or six groups of three and one group of two.

3. Repeat the material to yourself several times. Writing the material also helps.

4. Space your learning into several periods. Begin each new period by reviewing what you have previously memorized to keep it firmly planted in your memory.

5. Relate material you are learning to familiar ideas, persons, symbols and other things that are already firmly planted in your memory. For example, you can probably recall roughly what the map of Italy looks like, because it's shaped like a boot. Can you do the same for Yugoslavia?

6. Arrange ideas to be learned into a formula system or code word to aid your recall. For example, advertising teachers use the code word AIDA for "arouse Attention, create Interest, stimulate Desire and move to Action." Another example is the five-step study method called SQ3R which stands for Survey, Question, Read, Recite, Review.

7. Use spare moments, such as waiting time, for

memorizing. Carry note cards in your pocket for quick and easy referral.

I used those seven guidelines to overcome my two greatest memory challenges. In order to get my Ph.D. degree I had to pass exams in translating two foreign languages (French and German) into English. I had had no previous exposure to German and the French I knew was limited to spelling my name and reading New Orleans street signs. Nevertheless, I passed both of those tests six weeks after starting from scratch. I started out by buying the appropriate vocabulary cards (a thousand of them) and a set of graded readers. Each day I read for one hour in the reader and learned thirty new words from the vocabulary cards. Before learning new words I would review the words previously learned to reinforce my recall. At the end of five weeks I had learned all one thousand words and my reading and translating proficiency was well underway. The last week was reserved for polishing and reviewing. I passed both exams with flying colors.

If you use some of the modern memory aids, known as mnemonics, you will be able to amaze yourself and others with memory feats. With proper training almost anyone can learn to look through a shuffled deck of cards and remember them in order, meet fifty people and instantly recall their names, or recall over one hundred phone numbers. If you want more information on memory improvement, there are several good books on the subject, including Dr. Kenneth Higbee's *Your Memory*.

DEAL WITH TRIVIA IN BATCHES

All of us are plagued with a number of necessary minor tasks that must be done in the near future. Examples of these are paying bills, running errands, shopping, housework, yard work, minor repairs, correspondence, reading and making telephone calls. Attacking these tasks in a random fashion is one sure way to work more and accomplish less.

One way to keep trivia from hindering your effectiveness is to organize the tasks into batches and handle a batch at a time. Try to run several errands at one time. Go to the grocery, bank, car wash and filling station in one trip. Do several household chores in sequence, or combine several if possible. Save up your bills and pay them all at a certain time each month. Try to make telephone calls and write letters in batches. Trivia sessions are an effective method of preventing the minor things in your life from hindering your accomplishment of major goals.

PROBLEM-SOLVING STRATEGY

As you realize by now, planning and goal setting are basically a process of decision making, and decision making is problem solving. Organizing your approach to a problem puts you halfway toward solving it. The following general guidelines will help you achieve a basic readiness to meet and penetrate all roadblocks to success.

Don't Needlessly Complicate Your Problems

We live in an age of technological sophistication with trips to the moon, electronic brains and nuclear

74

power. Complexity is the norm. As a result, we have come to expect complexity in all facets of life. There appears to be an unwritten rule in our society that nothing has the right to be simple anymore. All too often when given the choice between a simple and complex solution to a problem, many of us opt for the latter. The story of using five men to change a light bulb (one to hold the bulb and four to turn the man on the ladder) makes us chuckle. But like most good humor it carries an underlying message containing some truth. As you try to solve a problem, look first for a simple satisfactory solution. It may save you a great deal of time.

Approach the Problem Creatively

Often our problem-solving ability is hindered by being locked into a particular way of viewing the problem. Many of us have heard the story of the truck being stuck in an underpass. A team of engineers was called out to decide how to dislodge the truck. True to their profession, they took an engineering approach to solving the problem and began making a series of complex stress calculations. A small boy standing by asked one of the engineers, "Hey mister, why don't you let the air out of the tires?" Immediately the problem was solved.

The more ways we allow ourself to view a problem, the better the odds of our finding a satisfactory solution.

Alex F. Osborne has a checklist for new ideas to stimulate your creative abilities. You may find the checklist helpful, as I have, when confronted with problem solving:

75

Could we . . .

1. Modify?
   _____ what to add
   _____ more time, greater frequency
   _____ stronger, higher, longer, thicker
   _____ duplicate, multiply, exaggerate

2. Minimize?
   _____ what to subtract
   _____ smaller, condense
   _____ omit, streamline, split up
   _____ lower, shorten, lighten

3. Substitute?
   _____ other process, ingredient, material
   _____ other place, other approach or form of
   approach

4. Rearrange?
   _____ interchange components
   _____ other sequence, schedule, pattern, layout
   _____ other person

5. Reverse?
   _____ transpose positive and negative
   _____ try opposite, turn backward or upside
   down
   _____ reverse roles

6. Combine?
   _____ uses, purposes, ideas, approaches

7. Put to Other Uses?
   _____ new ways to use
   _____ other uses if modified
   _____ what else is like this?

William James once said, "Genius means little more than the faculty of perceiving in an unhabitual way."

Whether you choose to use Osborne's checklist, brainstorm or whatever, it generally helps to try and see things from a different perspective.

Distinguish Between Urgency and Importance

When Dwight Eisenhower became President he tried to arrange his administration so that only urgent and important matters were called to his attention. Everything else was to be delegated to lower echelons. However, he discovered that urgency and importance seldom appear together. This concept also applies to our lives. Important things are seldom urgent and urgent things are seldom important. The urgency of fixing a flat tire when you are late for an appointment is much greater than remembering to pay your auto insurance premium, but its importance is, in most cases, relatively small.

Unfortunately, many of us spend our lives fighting fires under the tyranny of the urgent. The result is that we ignore the less urgent but more important things in life. It's a great effectiveness killer.

When you are faced with a number of problems to solve, ask yourself which are the important ones and make them your first priority. If you allow yourself to be governed by the tyranny of the urgent, your life will be one crisis after another. You'll be very active and may even be the busiest beaver around. However, someday you may wake up to find you've been building your dam on an empty lake.

Try to Anticipate Potential Crises

Doctors tell us that the best medicine is preventive medicine. You don't have to concern yourself with curing an illness if you don't have it. Thus, you take precautionary measures designed to maintain your health, such as getting enough rest, proper diet, exercise, vaccines and so on.

General problem-solving operates in much the same way. If you anticipate crises and take steps to prevent or deal with them, you will be wisely investing your time. Things seldom evolve to the crisis level without some warning. A little foresight and preventive maintenance can insure that you spend your time achieving your goals rather than reacting to crises.

Put Your Subconscious to Work

Some of our greatest problem-solving ability lies somewhere beneath our level of awareness Often we have trouble coming up with solutions to problems simply because we are pressing ourselves too hard for an answer. The anxiety and tension we create by agonizing for a solution cripple our creative abilities, as well as needlessly wasting time.

Some years ago, when I first entered graduate school, I agonized over what I would choose to write my doctoral thesis on. Although I wouldn't need to decide for at least two years, the thought of a thesis topic plagued me because I had never done one before. The idea of additional coursework and examinations was of no worry. I had been through all that before and felt confident of capable performance.

The more I pressed myself for a topic, the more anxious I became, and my thesis topic ideas remained nil. One day I mentioned this to one of my professors and he suggested that I simply forget about it and concentrate on the work at hand. "Turn the problem over to your sub-conscious," he said, "and let it work for you. When you get ready to tackle that thesis, your subconscious will have a topic for you. Most important decisions are usual-ly made at the subconscious level."

I took his advice and it really worked. Six months before I was ready to tackle the thesis a topic idea came to me. The value of subconscious decision-making was one of the greatest lessons I learned in graduate school.

CHAPTER 4

Making Every Day Count

"Many people assume that they can probably find many ways to save time. This is an incorrect assumption for it is only when you focus on spending time that you begin to use your time effectively."

—Merrill Douglass

"Where did the week go? I've been working like a demon from dawn till dusk and all I have to show for my effort is exhaustion."

"The main thing that blocks my getting ahead is that it takes all my time just to stay even."

"I have so much to do that I feel lost and overwhelmed. It's like someone just handed me a bucket and told me to go bail out the Mississippi River."

All of us are given the same amount of time in a given day, week or month. However, we have only to look around us to see that some of us get a great deal more mileage from our time than others. In this chapter, we will concern ourselves with two facets of time: how to account for it, and how to schedule for the effective use of it.

Do you really know how you spend your time? Most

of us think we do but the truth is that most of us don't. The plain fact about our use of time is that it is mostly a matter of habit. Most habits are timesavers because they allow us to do things without having to stop and think. However, many habits are useless practices that needlessly dissipate our time. Since we practice these habits without much thought, it follows that we aren't aware of most of them unless we make a conscious effort to discover them.

Most of us would prefer not to get to know ourselves too well. It's much easier to bury our heads in the sand than to observe and account for our behavior. To face ourselves and make an objective appraisal of our use of time takes a tremendous amount of courage. However, if you are willing to do it for one week, you will undoubtedly find it a beneficial experience.

The following exercise will reveal many things to you about what you *really* do with your time and your life. In this exercise, you take a one-week inventory of how you spend your time. I want to emphasize that this is not a "time nut" exercise telling you to account for every minute. All I ask is that you record how you spend the bulk of each half-hour of your life for one week. That's not so bad, is it?

From this exercise you will get a good, objective look at yourself. Not all of the disclosures will be to your liking. But realize that by having the courage to recognize your bad habits you greatly increase the odds of reducing and eliminating them. You will be taking a giant step toward working smart by trying to discover and reduce time-wasting behavior.

The following are step-by-step instructions on how to perform a time-inventory analysis. After the inventory, you will be considering some important questions whose answers will point the way to better use of your time.

HOW TO PERFORM A ONE-WEEK TIME ANALYSIS

1. Begin by preparing a time inventory statement like that of Figure. 2. This hypothetical statement is for Mr. I. M. Effective, a thirty-five-year-old sales executive,

Exhibit 2
Weekly Time Log And Summary Analysis Sheet

Time	Mon	Tue	Wed	Thu	Fri	Sat	Sun	Activity	Total Hours
7:00								1. Commuting To & From Work	
7:30								2. Meetings	
8:00								3. Telephone Calls	
8:30								4. Reading, Paper Work & Correspondence	
9:00								5. Aiding Subordinates	
9:30								6. Drop-In Visitors	
10:00								7. Seeing the Boss	
10:30								8. Travel on the Job	
11:00								9. Calling on Customers	
11:30								10. Miscellaneous Job Activities	
12:00								11. Grooming and Personal Care	
12:30								12. Eating	

Exhibit 2 Weekly Time Log And Summary
Analysis Sheet Continued

Time	Mon	Tue	Wed	Thu	Fri	Sat	Sun	Activity	Total Hours
1:00								13. Sleeping	
1:30								14. Cooking	
2:00								15. Laundering	
2:30								16. House Cleaning	
3:00								17. Yardwork and Household Maintenance	
3:30								18. Grocery Shopping	
4:00								19. Other Shopping	
4:30								20. Paying Bills	
5:00								21. Child Care Activities	
5:30								22. Religious Activity	
6:00								23. Family Outings	
6:30								24. Family Communication	
7:00								25. Miscellaneous Family Activity	
7:30								26. Radio, Music Listening	
8:00								27. Television Viewing	
8:30								28. Leisure Reading	
9:00								29. Hobbies	
9:30								30. Spectator Sports and Recreation	
10:00								31. Participant Sports	
10:30								32. Leisure Travel	

Exhibit 2 Weekly Time Log And Summary
Analysis Sheet Continued

Time	Mon	Tue	Wed	Thu	Fri	Sat	Sun	Activity	Total Hours
11:00								33. Parties and Socializing	
11:30								34. Miscellaneous Leisure Activities	
12:00								35. Other Activities	

husband and father of two children. Mr. Effective's wife is also employed outside the home, so Mr. Effective shares the domestic duties.

First, list about thirty of your major weekly activities. Then classify them into five or six major groups. Figure 2 shows job activities, personal activities, family activities, leisure and other activities, but your categories and activities may be totally different from Mr. Effective's.

After you feel you have enumerated and organized a sufficient number of categories, number each activity consecutively and prepare a four-column time record next to each, as shown in Figure 2.

2. Estimate how much time you spend on each activity per week to the nearest half-hour and record that figure in column 1, Estimated Weekly Time.

3. Next, prepare a weekly time log and summary analysis sheet (Figure 3), listing the activities on your time inventory statement.

4. For the next week, keep the time log and summary analysis sheet with you at all times. At every half-hour, record the number of the activity in which you have been engaged in the appropriate space of the analysis sheet. For example, if Mr. Effective spends from 7:00 to 7:30

Exhibit 3—Weekly Planner

Time	Sunday	Monday	Tuesday	Wednesday	Thursday	Friday	Saturday
8:00							
8:30							
9:00							
9:30							
10:00							
10:30							
11:00							
11:30							
12:00							
12:30							
1:00							
1:30							
2:00							
2:30							
3:00							
3:30							
4:00							
4:30							
5:00							
5:30							
EVE.							

#1 GOAL _____ WEEK OF _____

A.M. on Monday dressing for work, he would record the number 11 in the square reserved for Monday, 7:00.

5. At the end of the week, all of the time squares should have a number in them. The task now is to tally the number of times each activity appears. For example, if Mr. Effective's sheet has activity 3 listed thirteen times on his time sheet, this means he spent thirteen half-hours

or approximately six- and-a-half hours on the telephone at work. Thus Mr. Effective would enter 6.5 in the Total Hours column of the analysis sheet next to telephone calls. Continue tallying all categories and totaling the number of hours until there is a number (it may be zero) next to each activity in the Total Hours column.

6. Go back to the time inventory statement and record the Total Hours figures on the summary analysis sheet in the Actual Weekly Time column.

7. Fill in the Variance column on the inventory statement by subtracting Actual Weekly Time from Estimated Weekly Time. If you get a negative variance, it means you spent more time than you estimated on a given activity. If you get a positive variance, you spent less time than you estimated on a given activity.

8. Complete the Percentage of Actual Time column on the inventory statement for each activity. To do this use the following formula:

$$\% \text{ Actual Time} = \left(\frac{\text{Actual Weekly Time}}{168} \right) \times 100$$

9. Check your figures. The Actual Weekly Time column should add up to 168 hours and the Percentage of Actual Time should add up to approximately 100 percent. There may be some slight discrepancy from rounding off. If so, don't worry about it. The purpose of this exercise is to show where your time goes; it isn't an exercise in precision.

10. Go back to the subtotals for each group of activities and calculate them. Then construct a summary statement of the categories to give you a broader picture of how you spend your time. Mr. Effective's summary statement might look like Figure 4.

Once you have completed the time inventory and have become thoroughly familiar with the data, your next step is to use this information to help you toward better time use in the future. No doubt you found some real surprises, and not all of them were pleasant.

Figure 4

	estimated weekly time	actual weekly time	variance	percentage of actual time
Total Job Activities	45	50	–5	29.8
Total Personal Activities	45	40	5	23.8
Total Family Activities	32	46	–14	27.4
Total Leisure Activities	40	27.5	12.5	16.4
Other Activities	6	4.5	1.5	2.6
	168	168	0	100

The task now is to be scrupulously honest with yourself when performing the following exercise.

Take several sheets of paper, your time inventory statement and your written goals, and go where you will be alone and undisturbed. After careful consideration, write yourself some answers to the following questions:

1. How did I waste my time? What can be done to prevent or reduce time waste in the future?

2. How did I waste other people's time? Whose time did I waste? How can I prevent this from happening?

3. What activities am I now performing that can be reduced, eliminated or given to someone else to do?

4. What did other people do that wasted my time? Can anything be done to reduce or eliminate future occurrences? If so, what?

5. What did I do that was urgent but unimportant?

6. What did I do that was important in light of my goals?

7. Am I spending my time pursuing those things that are important to me? If not, why not? If so, how?

The answers to these questions should provide you with plenty of ideas that will enable you to make better use of your time. It's also an excellent idea to make a regular practice of taking a one-week time inventory every six months. It's much easier the second time around. You know how to do it and the surprises are fewer. You will probably find an improvement in your effectiveness after making a conscious effort at planning and goal setting. New bad habits can be readily uncovered and eliminated before they become deeply ingrained. As Samuel Johnson remarked, "The chains of habits are too weak to be felt until they are too strong to be broken." A periodic time inventory gives you a better-than-even chance of breaking those chains.

REPLACING OLD HABITS WITH NEW ONES

Somerset Maugham once said, "The unfortunate thing about this world is that good habits are so much easier to give up than bad ones." He might also have mentioned that old habits are easier to cling to than new ones are to adopt. Inertia makes change difficult. Turning the momentum in favor of new habits is not impossible, but it is difficult. What it requires can be summed up in two words: will power.

89

Almost a century ago the great American psychologist William James wrote a scientific paper on how to develop good habits and break bad ones. Time has not diminished the value of what James had to say. He lists three key points to follow in replacing new habits with old:

First, launch the new habit with strength and commitment. Devise a new routine to contrast with the old. Tell your friends or announce the change publicly. If you decide to lose ten pounds this month, tell everyone you plan to do so and how you plan to do it. This will build up your momentum and quell your temptation to buy that banana split. Every time you feel like going to the refrigerator you will think of all those people you made a commitment to.

James's second recommendation is to practice the new habit without exception until it is firmly rooted. Any lapse in practicing the new habit only gives the momentum back to the old one. It's much like having to start all over, and getting started is the hardest part. The more quickly a habit can be instilled, the greater are the chances of its becoming permanent. A reformed alcoholic will serve as a living testament to the value of James's second recommendation.

Finally, James recommends that we put our new habits into use at the earliest possible opportunity. Waiting until next month to start getting up an hour earlier, or to save for a new house, or to quit smoking only increases the odds that it will never get done. Good habits are acquired and strengthened by practice, not by procrastination. James put it this way: "A tendency to act becomes effectively ingrained in us only in proportion to the frequency with which the actions actually occur. When a resolve or fine glow of feeling is allowed to evaporate without bearing practical fruit, it is worse than a chance lost; it works so as to positively hinder the discharge of future resolutions and emotions."

One great aid to overcoming time-wasting habits is to acquire the habit of scheduling. Without further delay, let's look at some ideas that will enable you to work less and accomplish more through effective scheduling.

KEYS TO EFFECTIVE SCHEDULING

Like all other planning, effective scheduling is best done on paper. A good scheduling tool to use is the weekly planner (Figure 5). You can see an entire week laid out before you and get a better grasp of how it should be planned. It also provides a place for listing a top goal that is to be achieved during the week.

What type of schedule form you use is a personal choice. What matters most is that you use one that is suited to your lifestyle and tastes. Some of us schedule quite effectively with a simple desk calendar with two pages for each day. For others, a large monthly wall calendar with ample writing space by each date suffices. Some like to use a combination of schedules, one monthly, one weekly and one daily. Choose a style that you feel comfortable with. Being overly organized is no virtue, and when carried to extremes can be as crippling as total chaos.

Block Out Planning Time

Be sure to set aside a period of each day for thinking, reflecting and planning. Consider it a quiet time for

Figure 5 Weekly Planner

Time	Sun.	Mon.	Tues.	Wed.	Thurs.	Fri.	Sat.
8:00							
8:30							
9:00							
9:30							
10:00							
10:30							
11:00							
11:30							
12:00							
12:30							
1:00							
1:30							
2:00							
2:30							
3:00							
3:30							
4:00							
4:30							
5:00							
5:30							
EVE.							

 # 1 GOAL _____ **WEEK OF** _____

you to organize your thoughts about where you're going and how today will help you get there. For most of us this is best accomplished as the first item of the day. For others, it is best scheduled in the evening or as the last item on the agenda of the workday.

Whatever time of day you set aside for planning, just be sure you do it. It will repay you many times over.

Never tell yourself that you are too busy to plan. Probably one of the reasons you're so busy is that you didn't take time to plan. You've created a vicious circle for yourself. It's much like the proverb "He who rides a tiger can never dismount." Even if you can spare only five or ten minutes a day for planning, you will find the investment a worthwhile one.

Block Out Committed Time

After allowing time for planning, block out on your schedule all time that you have no control over. Such items as medical and dental appointments, meetings, out-of-town trips, classes or workshops and your job are examples of committed time.

This blocking off of committed time is often an exercise in frustration. When you are able to have the whole week or month laid out in front of you, it can be very exasperating to see how much of your immediate future is not yours. Don't let it upset you. That's only another way to waste your time. Instead, resolve to do something about it in the future. Remember, it's your life.

Put Important Deadlines on Your Schedule

In chapter 2, I pointed out that a goal should have a deadline if it's going to be a goal. Consequently, scheduling should take deadlines for goal achievement into account. Deadlines aid the scheduling process when handled in the following manner:

1. Determine the deadline target date and mark it on your schedule.

2. Estimate the amount of time you will need to complete the task at hand. Remember Murphy's Law. Just as the government takes its share of your money, Murphy will get his share of your time.

3. Once you have estimated how much time a task will consume, work back from the deadline and block off some remaining hours to devote to the task. This will also tell you the latest possible date you can expect to start the task and successfully meet the deadline.

Design a Flexible Schedule

Life is and always will be full of surprises. We can always expect the unexpected to come along and disrupt the best of plans. The only way to deal with the unexpected is to budget time for it. Failure to give ourselves breathing room in scheduling is where most of us make our greatest scheduling error. If we insist on running on a tight schedule, we are inviting the unexpected to raise havoc and destroy our scheduling efforts. Besides, tight schedules aren't much fun for most of us.

In scheduling, I've found this rule of thumb works for me: Estimate how much time you think a given activity or task will take and multiply it by 1.25. Thus, if I think a dental appointment will take an hour, I allow an hour and fifteen minutes on my schedule. If I think it will take four hours to prepare a lecture, I schedule five. If the task is something I'm totally unfamiliar with or have never done before, I estimate the time and multiply it by 1.5. Another excellent rule of thumb is to schedule only fifty percent of your time.

Block Out Time For Recreation and Diversion

In the words of Evan Esar, "All work and no play makes Jack a dull boy—and Jill a wealthy widow." It is bizarre that a recommendation of blocking out time for relaxation and recreation has to be mentioned. Yet we have only to look around us to see how many people cease to function fully when away from the job. Workaholics are usually very ambitious individuals who are willing to pay any price to get to the top. Unfortunately, what many of them fail to realize is that their compulsion to work can hinder their job effectiveness. By not taking time to get away from it all, compulsive workers lose the long-range perspective necessary for real success. They fail to see the forest for the trees.

The more stressful the work, the greater the need for frequent diversion and recreation. Many of our Presidents were noted for their recreational pursuits. Eisenhower was an avid golfer and Kennedy loved water sports. The vast pressures of such an office make it imperative that these men be at their best when on the job. If you look at the total picture of highly successful people, you will generally find a great deal more to their lives than their jobs. They may live to work, but they also live for a great deal more.

Make it a point to rediscover your nonvocational self and block out time to do so. Develop some outside interests or hobbies. It doesn't really matter what they are as long as you enjoy them and they allow you to escape mentally and/or physically. For some this may be tennis, while for others it may be collecting stamps or rocks. My present hobbies are talking on my amateur radio station (K5ML) to people around the world, and teaching my cats to do tricks (one of them can turn out the light). Both hobbies are a welcome change of pace from the enjoyable but lonely discipline of writing.

You will also find your effectiveness improved by allowing for breaks during your workday. What is best in terms of the number and length of breaks depends on the job and your individual makeup. When I was a student and when I am writing, I found the 50/10 system to be very effective. During each hour, I write or study fifty minutes and relax ten. If I go much beyond an hour without a break, I tend to lose my edge and the quality of my work suffers. On other jobs I have had, I rarely have felt the need to take a break.

To get the most from your breaks, experiment with various sytems until you find one that harmoniously combines comfort and results. The important thing to remember is that diversion is necessary for increased effectiveness as well as enjoyment. When speaking about overworked executives, Clarence Randall said it best: "Pity the overworked executive! Behind his paperwork ramparts he struggles bravely with a seemingly superhuman load of responsibilities. Burdened by impossible assignments, beset by constant emergencies, he never has a chance to get organized. Pity him—but recognize him for the dangerous liability he is."

Avoid Overcommitment—Learn to Say No

The artist James Whistler believed that the secret to successful painting was knowing what not to put on canvas. Similarly, your success at working smart depends on knowing what not to do. Master the ability of knowing how and when to say no, and half the battle is won.

Overcommitment is one of the most frequent ways we dilute our effectiveness. As I pointed out in Chapter 1, devoting a little of yourself to everything means you aren't able to commit a great deal of yourself to anything. You are left unable to concentrate on the important goals with the highest payoffs. Unfortunately, many of us just don't know how to refuse a request for our time when we could be putting it to better use. We usually say yes for two reasons: We are afraid someone else will have a lesser opinion of us, or a request for our help indulges our ego by giving us a feeling of power. Please don't misunderstand me—I'm not against helping people. What I'm referring to are the times we say yes when we know it is in our best interests to say no. When you say yes because of a need for approval, you are in effect saying to yourself that someone else's opinion of you is more important than your opinon of yourself. Saying yes to indulge your ego is the ammunition of martyrs. The hidden message is "You owe it all to me," with the emphasis on owe. It's a covert way of obligating others.

Make it a point to politely and directly refuse requests that are not in your own best interests. Learning to say no is like learning to swim. You increase your proficiency with practice.

The following guidelines will help you improve your ability to say no. The proper application of this most negative word can have very positive consequences in helping you effectively manage your time.

1. Say no rapidly before people can anticipate that you may say yes. Answers such as "I don't know" or "Let me think about it" only get people's hopes up. A delayed no only increases the chances of animosity.

2. Realize that you have the right to say no. You

don't have to offer a reason every time you turn down someone's request.

3. Offer your refusals politely and pleasantly. There's no need to be defensive—it's your right to say no.

4. Offer a counterproposal if you think it's appropriate and the request is a valid one. "I can't sit in for you at the meeting this afternoon, Joe, but I'll answer your telephone while you're out." Such an approach softens your refusal.

If knowing what not to do is such an important aspect of working smart, it seems only fitting that we should have a not-to-do list. I'm not saying you should sit down every day and make another list. Rather, I have compiled a list of things better left undone.

LeBoeuf's Not-to-Do List

1. All low-priority items—unless the high-priority items have been completed.

2. Any task whose completion is of little or no consequence. When you have something to do ask yourself the worst thing that could happen if you don't do it. If the answer isn't too bad, then don't do it.

3. Anything that you can give to someone else to do.

4. Anything just to please others because you fear their condemnation or you want to put them in your debt.

5. Thoughtless or inappropriate requests for your time and effort.

6. Anything others should be doing for themselves. When you find yourself working hard and accom

plishing little, remember the not-to-do list. It may help you in defining the problem.

Make the Most of Prime Time

Prime time is the time of day when you are at your best in performing a given task. You will find you can accomplish more with less effort if you schedule important tasks at the time of day when you perform them best.

Just what is prime time depends upon the person and the job. If you have a task requiring solitude and concentration, schedule it for the time of day at which you concentrate best. For many of us this is before 9 A.M., whereas others may concentrate best late in the evening. If the task involves others, try to avoid scheduling in the morning if you are a less-than-sociable morning person. I have one close friend who is barely a functioning human being before 3 P.M. He seems to be at his best between 10 P.M. and 2 A.M. Fortunately he has a career in broadcasting that enables him to take advantage of late-night prime time.

Through trial-and-error scheduling you can discover your prime time for a given task. For example, when I began writing I tried picking up the pencil at various times of the day. I found that in the morning my ideas were good, but I had trouble getting them on paper. I found the early afternoon to be my period of highest writing productivity and evenings the poorest. Therefore, I arrange my schedule to think about the current topics I'm writing on early in the morning. I jot down the ideas and put them aside. Then I tend to the day's other activities until early afternoon, when I write. It's a schedule that allows me to write with more enjoyment and less effort.

Look for Ways to Capitalize on Committed Time

In scheduling a given day, you block out time for certain essentials such as showering, dressing and commuting to and from work. However, sometimes you can put committed time to a second use. For example, one friend of mine, working toward a Master of Business Administration degree, studies while showering, dressing and driving to work. He does this by first recording his notes from class on a cassette tape recorder and then playing them back in the morning. Another friend of mine, a salesman, uses commuting time to memorize the names of his customers and salient details about each individual. He also uses a cassette recorder.

Another type of committed time we can put to further use is waiting time. Most of us simply write off the time we spend waiting for the doctor, the dentist or the hair stylist. However, with a little effort we can squeeze all sorts of activities into these minutes. While waiting for an appointment you can plan your weekend, update your goals or your to-do list, do isometric exercises, pay bills, meditate, write letters, or you can simply use this time to relax.

Also, there are plenty of major projects that you can nibble away at with occasional spare moments. You can work on knitting a sweater, planning your dream home or outlining that novel you always promised to write. With a little imagination you can easily come up with plenty of ideas.

Another type of committed time is shopping time.

Going to the grocery, downtown or to the shopping center can consume huge amounts of time, most of which is unproductive. The best way to make effective use of shopping time is to minimize it, and this means shopping during periods of least activity. Avoid supermarkets and shopping centers on weekends. Arrange your schedule to shop during weekdays or evenings. Do your banking in the morning and avoid the lunch-hour crowd. If you find yourself stuck in a line, be prepared to have something to do. Carry a memory list and resolve to memorize such things as frequently called telephone numbers or names and important facts about customers.

Another good way to capitalize on committed time is to carry three-by-five cards or a pad of paper for jotting down ideas that come to you. Better yet, carry a pocket dictating-unit or a miniature cassette recorder.

Most of us operate with a time perspective of hours, days and weeks. It's the minutes and the lifetimes that we seem to be most apt to ignore. With a little thought we can make the most of both.

A FINAL THOUGHT ON SCHEDULING

As you read over the ideas I have presented on scheduling, you may be thinking to yourself, "I can't always do that." Rest assured, none of us can. Life is far from perfect. On many occasions, you may not be able to make your schedule as flexible as you would like. Unfortunately, the nature of your job may not permit you to use the prime-time concept to your greatest advantage. None of us are able to apply all of these ideas all of the time—and wouldn't life be dull if we could!

The point is that all of us can apply all these concepts some of the time. The more we are alert to and apply these ideas, the more we will be able to accomplish with a given amount of time and effort. And that's what working smart is all about.

CHAPTER 5

New Attitudes for Effectiveness

"A diamond is a chunk of coal that made good under pressure."

—*Classic Crossword Puzzles*

Life is an attitude. Of that much I am sure. Insasmuch as work is such a large part of living, it follows that how we spend our time and energy is also a matter of attitude. Tell me what you think and how you feel and I'll tell you who you are. How hard we work and how much or little we accomplish is largely governed by thoughts and feelings.

In the process of going through life, we gather beliefs about our thoughts and feelings and, like the work tapes, many of these beliefs are false. We have been propagandized to believe that our feelings are something mysterious, uncontrollable and independent of our thoughts. The notion that "really living" means a life of highly uncontrollable emotional experiences is another concept we are bombarded with. We are taught to be responsible for the feelings and attitudes of others. We learn that the "conscientious, good person" is someone who feels guilty about his past and worries about his future and the future of others. It's a wonder anything gets accomplished with the massive amount of time and energy that is needlessly wasted each day on these myths.

YOU'RE BETTER THAN YOU THINK!

There's just no doubt about it. When it comes to self-evaluation, we simply sell ourselves short. You are smarter, stronger, more creative and more talented than you believe you are. The vast majority of us never come anywhere near applying the reservoir of potential within us. Why this is I cannot say for sure, but in my opinion our greatest limiting factor is our concept of who we are.

Don't take my word for it. Talk to Ohio State's Woody Hayes, one of the winningest coaches in college football. During a television interview, Hayes remarked that he is certain that all of us are better than we believe we are, and that he views his basic job as a coach as taking a young man for four years and convincing him that he's better than he thinks.

Coach Paul "Bear" Bryant of Alabama echoed Woody's sentiments from a different perspective. "There are several kinds of football players," Bryant once theorized. "There are those who have it and know it, those who have it and don't know it, those who haven't got it and know it, and those who haven't got it and don't know it. Those who haven't got it and don't know it have won us more games than anybody."

It appears that our self-image is at the core of all of

our behavior and its preservation is a motive for practically everything we do. We tenaciously cling to any ideas we believe about ourselves, for better or for worse. What this does is create a self-fulfilling prophecy in which our behavior confirms our self-image. Believe that you are shy, aggressive, worthwhile, friendly, intelligent or whatever, and your behavior will tend to support your concept of who you are.

We cling to self-concepts and resist changes in them because they are our main contact with reality. To lose contact with oneself is indeed traumatic. Yet many things we believe about our inherent makeup are simply untrue or a rationalization. How many times have you heard someone say, "I'm sorry, but that's just the way I am"? The strongest motive in a person is not self-preservation but preservation of that person's self-image.

Strengthening your self-image is a key to increased effectiveness. In the final analysis, winners above all see themselves as winners. They may not win them all, but they sure win more than their share. Unfortunately, the self-fulfilling prophecy holds equally true for losers. It's much as Disraeli said: "We make our fortunes and we call them fate."

STRENGTHEN YOUR SELF-IMAGE

A stronger self-image gives us the "can do" power to climb to the highest summits and have energy to spare. Changing your self-image is tough but it can be done with a little will power and self-discipline. The following guidelines can help point the way toward helping you bolster your self-worth.

Put the Past in the Past

In the process of maturing we all encounter experiences that contribute to making up our self-image. Unfortunately, we are left clinging to erroneous ideas of our abilities and character traits. Those ideas that affect our work are such self-defeating statements as:

- I lack initiative.
- I don't express myself well.
- I can't handle responsibility.
- I'm not assertive.
- I'm not strong.
- I can't think clearly.
- I have to work twice as hard as most people.
- I rebel against authority.
- I'm lazy.
- I'm disorganized and undisciplined.
- I'll go crazy if I don't keep busy.
- I can't work without supervision.
- I'm not a good worker.
- I'm unworthy of an important position or promotion.
- I'm sarcastic and abrasive.

Many of the things we tell ourselves about ourselves are true only because we choose to believe they are. Or we behaved in an unsatisfactory manner in the past because we believed we were that way.

This trap can be beaten by putting the past in proper perspective. Yesterday is farther away than the last day of your life because yesterday will never come again.

Instead of saying "I'm unorganized" or "I lack initiative," say "I've chosen to be that way in the past but today is another story."

Then write yourself some goals designed to contradict those statements. If you've been telling yourself you lack initiative, start a new task or project that will increase your value to the company. Make a list of all the "I'ms" you believe about yourself, and then write a plan of action for proving yourself wrong. Follow through on your plans and you will soon have a lot of weight taken off your shoulders, as the ghosts of the past vanish.

Build on Your Strengths

Everyone's self-image is a mixture of both positive and negative qualities. Thus, in addition to rectifying negatives, you can enhance your self-image by dwelling on your present positive qualities and using them to best advantage.

Make a list of your positive traits and examples that prove you have these qualities. For instance, if you think you're good with interpersonal relationships, note the time you landed the company that important contract through your own personal charm, or the time you resolved a misunderstanding that prevented a valuable employee from resigning.

After you have listed your strengths, consider them in light of your goals. How can you use them to help you achieve your goals? Which ones will be most useful in this regard?

If you stop and take stock of your strengths, you will be amazed at how many good traits you have. Don't be modest and hold back. Build yourself up! Then resolve to make the most of your strengths. It's the psychological leverage of working smart.

Accept Yourself—Unconditionally

Never confuse your intrinsic worth with your external successes, failures, triumphs or tragedies. You are a perfectly valuable, worthwhile individual simply because you exist. It's okay to be you.

Conditionally accepting yourself is one way to insure that you will never be totally at peace with yourself. How many times have you thought "I'll be worthwhile when I graduate from school, get a driver's license, make $20,000 a year, own my own home, get promoted, pay off the mortgage, get a raise..." and so on? Yet no sooner do we reach one goal than there is another "I'll be okay when..." beckoning to us. You're okay now.

Don't Allow Others to Define Your Worth

Building your self-image on others' opinions of you is like building the foundation of a house on a bed of quicksand. Sooner or later it's bound to cave in. Unfortunately, we are taught from the cradle to the grave that behavior that results in the approval of others is the key to our personal happiness and well-being. Society sends out all sorts of messages, some subtle and others not so subtle, to insure that our behavior is other-directed. Women in particular are often victims of these messages. Practically all media advertising is based on the value of pleasing others. Over and over the message is "Buy the product and be accepted, loved, esteemed and more worthwhile." We are all happier when we enjoy the approval of others. However, we have magnified its importance so much that many of us tie it to our self-image.

By and large, people are fickle, and the one that loves and praises you today may not tomorrow. Whenever someone rejects, condemns or tries to belittle you, remember what Eleanor Roosevelt remarked: "No one can make you feel inferior without your consent."

It is also wise to refrain from letting others define your capabilities. Never let anyone tell you you're too old, too young, too lazy or too anything to accomplish what you want. If it seems possible to you and you want to do it, then move full speed ahead. As Emerson wrote, "Self-trust is the first secret of success."

Our world has experts on every corner telling people what they are and aren't capable of. And for every expert, there are at least a hundred people proving them wrong. John Kennedy couldn't be elected President because he was a Catholic and Jimmy Carter because he was a southerner. Once, when I was in high school, a counselor encouraged me to learn a trade after graduation because college would be "difficult, if not impossible" for me. Eight years later, I had a Ph.D. Robert Ringer's definition is my favorite: "An expert is merely a guy who knows all the reasons why you can't do something."

Put What You Want First

For years, we have been fed another social message and that is to subordinate our desires to those of others in order to achieve a better world. So we sacrifice our own needs for the good of our spouse, children, company, government or whatever. How unfortunate.

The problem with such a philosophy is that it ultimately breeds resentment on the part of all concerned. You don't help the poor by becoming one of them. You help them by keeping your own needs satisfied and helping them to help themselves.

Much the same is true for all of our other relationships. Positive selfishness is the prerequisite to forming good relationships with others. Until you feel good and self-satisfied about your own life, you have little to offer someone else to help theirs.

To quote from the Talmud: "Every man has the right to feel 'because of me the world was created.'" If you are burning with altruistic desire, I would suggest you adopt that viewpoint. You can't fill an empty bucket with a dry well. It's much as George Bernard Shaw said: "A man's interest in the world is only the overflow of his interest in himself."

ONLY YOU CONTROL YOUR THOUGHTS AND FEELINGS

Developing effective work attitudes begins with understanding your feelings and where they come from. Contrary to popular belief, your feelings are not a mystical, uncontrollable phenomenon that governs your behavior. Rather, your feelings are a product of your thought processes. How many times have you heard someone tell another to "stop feeling and start thinking" or something to that effect? In reality, that's an absurd statement because without thinking there is no feeling.

Only after you think about something do you choose how you will feel. For example, you're at work and someone tells you that the boss is very displeased with your performance and wants to see you this afternoon. Upon hearing this, you may choose to feel guilty, worry, be apathetic or forget it until you talk with the boss. The point is that until you got the message and had time to think about it, it was impossible for you to have any feelings concerning the matter.

110

Most of us don't believe that we can control our feelings but most of us know that with a little self-discipline we can control our thoughts. However, if we can control our thoughts, and feelings come from thoughts, then it logically follows that we can control our feelings.

An example of feelings are the attitudes we have toward the days of the week. Most of us feel a certain way on Mondays, another way on Fridays and so on. However, how would you know how to feel on Monday if you didn't know it was Monday? The simple fact is you wouldn't. Each Monday you wake up, think to yourself "It's Monday" and then make a decision on how to feel about it.

If we control our feelings, we choose to be happy, sad, guilty, worried, anxious or enthusiastic. Nobody makes us happy. We make ourselves happy and the same holds true for the other emotions we experience. Don't expect anyone to make you happy, enthusiastic, motivated or energetic about your work. That's your decision.

You may feel that being responsible for your own feelings seems rather awesome, but the truth is that such a philosophy takes a lot of pressure off you. If you accept the premise that each person must satisfy himself, then you aren't responsible for anyone's happiness but your own. Ralph Waldo Emerson put it nicely: "Most of the shadows of this life are caused by standing in one's own sunshine." With that thought in mind, let's take a look at some of the shadows that result in fatigue and frustration.

Guilt—a Bad Case of the "Shouldas"

Of all the effectiveness-killing emotions, guilt is absolutely the most useless. No amount of regret, remorse,

111

or bad feeling can change the past. However, guilt by definition is feeling bad and becoming immobile over that which has occurred or should have occurred earlier. You can rewrite history but you can't relive it.

If guilt is such a futile, irrational waste of time and energy, then why do we spend so much of our life being consumed by it? There are several answers.

First and foremost is the fact that we were fed large doses of guilt conditioning as children. Parents, teachers and religious institutions use guilt to regulate behavior. As children we were taught what behavior is right and wrong. Then we were told that our role was to feel good when we were right and bad when we were wrong. Such behavior and thinking is carried over into adulthood. As a result, we see guilt used in some form to regulate behavior in practically every institution and area of society.

However, there are several other reasons why we may choose to spend our efforts on guilt. Guilt is a tremendous cop-out for not being effective. If you're busy feeling guilty, you don't have to use the present to get something done.

Guilt gives you a perfect excuse for not changing yourself. You do something that isn't self-enhancing, "pay your dues" by feeling bad about it, and life goes on. You avoid the risks as well as the work that go with positive self-improvement. It's another application of the easy-way tape.

Guilt is a great way to hold others responsible for your behavior and your feelings, thus exonerating yourself from any wrongdoing. Such behavior often manifests itself in statements such as "See what they made me do," "If it weren't for them" and "Shame on you."

Finally, guilt is a good method of winning the approval and pity of others. By feeling guilty, you show the world what a wonderful, conscientious, caring person you are. Unfortunately, many of us would rather be pitied than fulfilled.

When applied to work, guilt usually results in what I call a case of the "shouldas." Symptoms of this malady can be seen in such statements as "I shoulda gotten approval before taking action," "I shoulda started that project earlier" and "I shoulda done everything on my to-do list." The fact is that you can't "shoulda" anything. The past is history. You can only learn from it and resolve to behave differently in the present and the future.

Many of us waste a great deal of our time and energy feeling guilty about what doesn't get done. A secretary once asked me how to get more done and I recommended a to-do list to her. I bumped into her several weeks later and asked how it was working out. She replied, "Oh, it really helped, but I had to give it up. I never got to finish the list and felt so bad that I went home each night with a headache." Upon hearing that, I explained that she didn't have to expect to complete the list and told her about the 80/20 rule.

"Oh! That's much better," she replied. "Why didn't you tell me this before?"

"I don't know," I said. "I guess I shoulda."

Guilt over what doesn't get done gives you a lifelong ticket to misery, because you will never get everything done. Expecting to get everything done is as futile as a dog chasing his tail. However, there is always enough time to do the important things. I read an anonymous

113

prayer that I feel has the proper perspective: "Lord, there's never enough time for everything. Help me to do a little less a little better."

Needless to say, guilt is one emotion we are better off without. The following are common-sense recommendations aimed at eliminating or at least minimizing the pangs of guilt:

1. Recognize the past for what it is. Write down ten things that you have done that you wish you hadn't. Then write down ten things that you didn't do that you wish you had. Give yourself five points for each item that feeling bad about will help. Your score? Zero!

2. Practice feeling guilty. Set aside fifteen or twenty minutes and find a past event to feel badly about. Now, get in there and feel guilty! Oh my God! Ain't it awful! If only I hadn't! That's what I should have done! Soon you will come to realize what an enormous drain on your energy guilt is. It will impress you with the need for saying good-bye to guilt.

3. List all the things you are avoiding doing by feeling guilty and resolve to do something about them. You can avoid accomplishing anything in life by feeling guilty about being lazy or lacking direction. Resolve to set your goals and spend your time achieving them rather than feeling guilty.

4. Accept your past mistakes and misfortunes and resolve to learn something from them. As a human being you have the right to be wrong.

5. Put the guilt wielders in their place. The world is filled with neurotic people who make it a practice to try to cast off their bad feelings on others. You need guilt wielders like you need plague or four years of bad crops.

Your only responsibility is to ignore these people or, better yet, get them out of your life.

In addition to guilt, there is another totally useless emotion that bears a strong resemblance to guilt. That emotion is . . .

Worry

Worry is the mirror reflection of guilt. Instead of fretting about the past, worriers think about all the terrible things that the future may hold. Guilt is past-oriented and worry is future oriented. Both insure that absolutely nothing worthwhile will be achieved in the present.

About worry, Mark Twain once remarked, "I've suffered a great many catastrophes in my life. Most of them never happened." The fact is that all our worries are fantasies. None of the things we worry about exist in the present and the vast majority will not exist in the future. Whatever does come to pass will certainly not be changed by worrying.

The psychological payoffs for worry are similar to those of guilt. Worrying is a great excuse for not being effective. How often have you heard someone say, "I'm just too upset and worried to concentrate on my job?" Robert Lee Frost once said, "The reason worry kills more people than work is that more people worry than work." Worry is work—hard work and totally unproductive at that.

Worry also shows everyone how much you care and how responsible you are. After all, it shows you're thinking about the future and not wasting time enjoying today.

Worrying is easier than changing. Instead of trying to build a better future by taking present action, you can simply worry about what might happen. For example, my friend Harry is a thirty-five-year-old alcoholic. Six nights out of every week he can be seen getting smashed in the neighborhood bar. Not surprisingly, Harry has high blood pressure, most of it probably due to his consumption of alcohol.

Harry is very worried about his heart. But has he curtailed his drinking? Not at all! Instead, he spends his days reading medical research journals in the library, taking his blood pressure and frequenting his doctor's office. Harry doesn't have a job although he is very bright and has a master's degree in one of the applied sciences. There is no financial reason for Harry to work. His wealthy father gives him a handsome monthly stipend which is more than enough to live and drink on. Harry did get a job several years back but quit after one day, claiming it was bad for his heart. Will Harry ever change? Not in the foreseeable future, if ever. Why should he go through the rigor of change when drinking and worrying are so easy?

Worry has one other payoff—it can get you loads of sympathy and pity. A professional worrier doesn't worry for nothing. He has all sorts of things to show for his efforts, like headaches, ulcers, backaches and various other real and imagined illnesses. Pity the poor worrier—and all your pity is probably just what he wants.

Worrying is something all of us could do less of, because any amount is too much. Here are some things you can do that will help you get worry out of your life:

1. Think back to a particular time in your life, be it

one, five, ten or twenty years ago. Make a list of all the things you worried about then. How many of them never came to pass? Most of them. How many did you prevent by worrying? None. How many actually happened but turned out to be blessings in disguise?

A professor, whom we shall call Roscoe, wasn't terribly happy in his job teaching in the university and continually worried about being fired. What would he do? How would he pay the bills and support his family? Sure enough, Roscoe's greatest dread came to pass and he was let go. A year later I ran into Roscoe and he was a changed man. One month after leaving the university he had landed a fine consulting job at double his previous salary. More importantly, he found the new job far more challenging and fulfilling. All of his worry about clinging to the security of academia had only held him back from a happier life. Roscoe's experience reminded me of an anonymous quote I once read: "Man cannot discover new oceans unless he has courage to lose sight of the shore."

2. Make a list of the worst things that have ever happened to you. Then ask yourself how many of them came as a total shock. Most of the real tragedies of this life are unanticipated, and what a blessing that is. You don't have a chance to worry about their occurring, and worry wouldn't prevent their occurrence anyway.

3. When you are worried about something, confront it head-on. Ask yourself, "What's the worst that could come from this?" When you answer that question, the need for worry usually vanishes.

4. Sit down and worry. Think of as many bad things as you can think of that could happen to you in the next twenty-four hours. For example, you could die, become permanently paralyzed, lose a loved one, your house

could burn down, etc. You will soon realize that the list could go on forever and that you simply don't have enough time to worry about it all. So why worry about anything?

5. Replace worrying with action planning. If you're so concerned with the future, then spend your time and energy making it better for you and your family. Set yourself some meaningful goals and go after them, starting now! If the goals are really meaningful to you, you'll have so much fun getting absorbed in pursuing them that you won't have the time or energy for worrying.

By eliminating guilt and worry, you rid yourself of two major effectiveness-killing emotions. However, there are two other dragons remaining to be slain. It seems that guilt and worry have teamed up to produce a third monster which is . . .

Fear of Failure

Stop for a moment and think of all the wonderful things in this world that never happened because someone feared failure and hadn't the courage to act. Think of all the books, songs and plays that were never written. Think of all those singers, musicians, painters and sculptors who never developed their talent because they were afraid someone would laugh. Think of all the great labor-saving inventions and cures for presently incurable diseases that were missed because someone was afraid to pursue his far-out theory. And finally, think of all the beautiful relationships that never blossomed because one or both parties feared rejection. This is only a fraction of the price we pay for indulging ourselves in the fear of failure.

The startling fact is that there is no such thing as failure. "Failure" is merely an opinion that a given act wasn't done satisfactorily. As a natural phenomenon it doesn't exist. Imagine, if you will, one honeybee saying to another, "They put me to work in the hive because I got a 'D' in pollenation." Better yet, can you imagine one squirrel telling another, "Max, you're a first-class climber, but your nutcracking is inadequate"? How ludicrous can you get? The fact is animals don't know what failure is. They simply do and enjoy. Failure doesn't stop them because it's totally off their map. If Max can't open a nut, he simply tries another. He doesn't wallow in self-pity or swear to subsist on tree bark for the rest of his life.

Like the other immobilizing emotions, choosing to be governed by the fear of failure has definite payoffs. Being ruled by fear of failure lets you take the easy way out. Rather than accepting the challenge of pursuing a meaningful goal, you can scratch it off your list and tell yourself that success is impossible or not worthwhile.

Reacting to a fear of failure also provides a false sense of safety and security. You can't lose a race you don't enter. Thus by not doing, you are spared the seemingly needless humiliation of failure. You'll never be a winner but you'll never be a failure either.

If you've ever met with less than success in the past (and who hasn't?), the fear of failure gives you a perfect excuse for not trying in the present or future. After all, what's the point in going to all that trouble for nothing?

Finally, by not trying to give yourself the luxury of becoming a critic. You can put your time and effort into being a spectator and ridiculing all those fools who are out there trying to succeed. The most vociferous critics are generally frustrated doers who are ruled by their own fear of failure.

Those who give in to their fears and choose the psychological payoffs overlook one major point. Failure is not a measure of success. In fact, as we already pointed out, failure isn't anything. In life, it isn't what you lose that counts, it's what you gain and what you have left.

If you find yourself immobilized due to fear of failure here are some ideas to help you overcome it:

1. Set your own standards of success. Remember that failure is arbitrary. Don't allow your life to be ruled by standards other than your own. You don't have to be president of the company because your father was or your wife wants you to be. It's your choice, not theirs.

2. Don't fall into the trap of success-failure thinking. If you set a goal and pursue it, evaluate your own performance in terms of degrees of success.

3. Don't feel you have to succeed or achieve excellence in everything you do. There's nothing wrong with a mediocre round of golf (at least that's what I keep telling myself) or a poor set of tennis, as long as you're having fun.

4. Meet your fear of failure head-on. Find something you would like to do but fear failure in, and do it. Even if you don't succeed to the degree you hope to, you won't have any regrets. After all, you will be doing what you want to do. It's better to feel sorry for the things you've done than to regret missed opportunities. All ventures involve risk, but not to venture is to waste your life.

5. If you do feel you have failed, recognize it as a learning experience that will make you wiser and contribute to later successes. Astute young politicians practice

this. They join a political race fully realizing they have no chance of winning. However, by throwing their hat in the ring, they get public exposure and learn the ropes of campaigning. All of the exposure and learning can some-day contribute to a victorious campaign. We can learn a great deal more from our failures than our successes, provided we avail ourselves of the opportunity.

6. Realize that meaningful success if rarely easy and is usually preceded by a struggle. However, it's those who have the will to see it through that make it. Most of us throw in the towel too soon, when hanging in there a little longer would do the job. In his book *The Art of Selfishness,* David Seabury strikes this analogy:

> In South Africa, they dig for diamonds. Tons of earth are moved to find a little pebble not as large as a little fingernail. The miners are looking for the diamonds, not the dirt. They are willing to lift all the dirt in order to find the jewels. In daily life, people forget this principle and become pessimists because there is more dirt than diamonds. When trouble comes, don't be frightened by the negatives. Look for the positives and dig them out. They are so valuable it doesn't matter if you have to handle tons of dirt.*

Last but not least is the final time and energy kill-er . . .

Anger

If anything good comes from severe anger and its by-products of hatred and bitterness, I've yet to see it. It certainly accomplishes nothing regardless of whether it's

*David Seabury, *The Art of Selfishness* (New York: Cornerstone Library, 1964), p. 180.

aimed at others, oneself or inanimate objects. In the final analysis, the angry person is saying, "The world and its people must live up to my expectations." Of course, such a demand is totally ridiculous. Anger starts wars and unless we learn to control it, anger may lead to the total extinction of humanity.

Like the other three immobilizing emotions, anger has its neurotic rewards. If you're angry at other things or people, then it's all their fault for not living up to your expectations. Therefore, you don't have to change.

Anger can get you loads of sympathy, attention and power over those who will allow you to manipulate them. "Poor George, he has such a terrible temper. It's really a shame, because he has such bad headaches, backaches and high blood pressure as a result. Let's just do what he wants. God forbid what might happen if he gets mad! And besides, it's not his fault that he's such a sensitive, intense and totally alive person."

Anger gives you license to go temporarily insane, thus exonerating you from responsibility for unsatisfactory behavior. You can tell yourself and others, "I don't know what came over me. I just lost my temper."

Finally, anger is an excuse for incompetence. You can blame your bad temper for your inability to think straight or take constructive action.

Of course, all of those payoffs are total wastes of time and energy. Getting out of your car and kicking the tires when you break down on the freeway isn't going to get you rolling again. However, the most self-destructive anger is that which is aimed at other people. The late Senator Hubert Humphrey put it best: "Bitterness takes too much energy and accomplishes nothing. It doesn't hurt the other person. You think you're sending out the rays of bitterness like laser beams, but they stay inside of you—consuming *you*."

We live in an angry age typified by high crime rates, petty bickering, broken homes and people suing each other at the drop of a hat. Whatever the reasons, there are lots of us who evidently feel that the solution to our problems is anger. How unfortunate.

You are best off if you can eliminate your anger completely. If you can't eliminate anger, here are some useful ideas for coping with it:

1. Vent your anger constructively. It isn't healthy to suppress anger but there are constructive alternatives to venting it. For example, you can work your frustrations out with a regular exercise program.

Sometimes a little anger can provide an additional spark to move you toward meeting your goals. For example, when I first started making plans to write this book I mentioned it to one of my colleagues at work. He laughed at the idea and said it would never get written, much less published. I went home and started writing that day. His negative reaction was just what I needed to get me moving. How can I ever thank him enough?

2. Take your work seriously, but not yourself. Ethel Barrymore put it best when she said, "You grow up the day you have your first real laugh at yourself." There is absolutely no future in taking life too seriously. Our mental institutions and prisons are filled with people who have.

Develop your sense of humor and use it frequently. It is impossible to laugh and be angry at the same time. A good sense of humor creates positive energy and prevents the negative emotions from clouding your life. Your life is a gift that you must give back to your creator one day. So enjoy it to the hilt and leave the long faces to those who are going to live forever.

3. Accept the fact that many things in life will not live up to your expectations. This is hardly a perfect world, and I don't know about you, but I'd feel terribly out of place if it were. Practice accepting those things in life you cannot change. Tolerance and serenity are great antidotes to anger.

4. Give your anger a rain check. If something bothers you count to ten or, better yet, tell yourself, "I'll get mad about this tomorrow." Postponing anger is a good way to minimize it. Spontaneously unloading your anger on your boss, spouse or secretary can escalate minor mishaps into major catastrophes. Postponing your anger can reduce the odds of that happening.

5. Realize that you don't have to get mad to take constructive action. Positive, enthusiastic emotions achieve fulfillment, making good use of time and creating energy rather than draining it.

Ridding yourself of guilt, worry, fear of failure and excessive anger can make you a new person. Suddenly you will find you have time, energy and abilities you never dreamed you had. Picture yourself as a container in which time and energy is stored and your time and energy as the liquid in the container. The negative emotions are holes in the bottom of the container. To the extent that you are able to plug up the holes, you will have more time and energy to do the things in life that are fulfilling to you. To carry the analogy one step further, the greater the pressure that is applied to the liquid, the faster it will drain out of the holes. This is also true with work. Best use of time and energy is made by taking the pressure off. However, before we can take the pressure off we have to know where the pressure *really* comes from.

EASING UP THE PRESSURE

In transactional analysis, mention is made of the harried worker. He or she may be an executive, clerk, housewife, teacher, doctor, farmer or whatever. However, no matter what the job is, the situation is the same. A harried worker is under the gun. He is constantly overworked and complains of having to do his job and everyone else's. He takes work home evenings and weekends. At work he is in constant motion and is very brief with associates, bosses and subordinates. He says yes to all requests for his time and energy, and may even brag of having not had a vacation in fifteen years. To him hard work and life are one, and he wears his hard-work image on his shirtsleeve as a merit badge for all to admire.

Sooner or later the pressures of living the harried life begin to take their toll and the harried hero begins to deteriorate. He still says yes to all requests, but he's no longer able to come through. His appearance becomes haggard and his eyes bloodshot with deep circles underneath. Illness and depression become frequent. Often the final chapter of the harried worker's life is an abrupt and unexpected one. It's very common to find a harried player slumped over his desk, dead of a heart attack and surrounded by his work. The pressures of his job were just too much for him. Right? Wrong!

The harried player, like everybody else, creates his own pressure. In the final analysis pressure, like happiness, anger, guilt, worry and fear, is internal. It's only when you choose to accept pressure that you have it. Everyone talks of hard work and the pressures of living in our society, but the fact is that when we are talking about pressure we are talking about what we do to ourselves. It's much like Pogo once said: "We has met the enemy and they is us."

There is something in virtually every chapter of this book that will indirectly help you reduce the pressure of work. However, the following ideas are presented to provide you with some pressure-free attitudes toward work.

Approach Your Work Relaxed

When I started playing golf I went to a pro for my first lesson. It turned out to be an education in much more than golf. The pro's instructions on how to swing a golf club left me with numerous things to think about every time I approached the ball. I had to think about my stance, my grip, my back swing, my hips, my follow-through, my head and so on. But the most important thing the pro said to do was to relax. He was right. If you concentrate too much on every detail of the swing, your body tenses up and you end up not hitting the ball or hitting it poorly. The pro called this overconcentration syndrome "paralysis by analysis." You can't be an effective golfer unless you can relax. An easy, well-coordinated swing is what gives you control over the ball.

Likewise, an easy, well-coordinated approach to your work is what enables you to be effective. If you find yourself terribly tense, stop and ask yourself what all that tension is accomplishing. Then slow down your pace.

Move calmly and deliberately towards your goals. The relaxed, easy-does-it approach is a deceptively powerful one. Remember, activity is not productivity.

When things do get hectic, one of the best tonics is to take a short pause and do nothing but totally relax, physically and mentally. If you find yourself overly tense in the middle of working, take a short pause and try this:

1. Assume a comfortable position sitting or reclining. Loosen any tight clothing.

2. Close your eyes and imagine yourself sitting by a calm lake or stream with a picturesque mountain view. Feel the pleasant warmth of the sunlight on your face as you visualize this scene of total tranquility. Empty your mind of all other thoughts.

3. Slowly let each part of your body go totally limp. Breathe deeply and concentrate on relaxing first your forehead and then your chin, neck, arms, torso, and legs, in that order. Think of your body as a balloon with the air escaping from it and falling completely depleted.

4. Remain in this totally relaxed state for ten minutes, or longer if you prefer. Remember that the keys to this exercise are total physical relaxation and emptying the mind of all thoughts and problems.

According to a group of Harvard medical researchers, relaxation breaks on the job tend to improve a worker's over-all health and job satisfaction by lowering blood pressure and frequency of headaches, and improving the ability to deal with others. This is one investment of time with a potentially high payoff.

Enjoy Your Work

You may be highly paid for what you do. Your job may come with tremendous vacation, sick-leave, hospitalization and retirement benefits. However, if you don't enjoy what you are doing, I question your success.

The most successful people I know are those who enjoy what they do while they are doing it. The real fun in life comes from total creative absorption in a task and not in the external rewards for doing it. When you enjoy your work, you feel a sense of harmony, purpose and comfort; and this sense of internal success will increase the odds of greater external rewards in the long run.

If you don't like your work, get out of it and find something you do enjoy. Obviously, all jobs have their pleasant and unpleasant aspects, but if you find the inherent nature of your work distasteful, you would be better off looking for greener pastures. Despite any present doubts you may have, I assure you you'll never regret it.

Recognize the Paradox of Perfection

The paradox of perfection is that by expecting perfection in yourself or others, you make a huge mistake. Most of us are immobilized by perfectionism more than we are aware of or are willing to admit. Our society has fed us large doses of the "be perfect" injunction. Those who appear more perfect than others are held up as a model for all to see. "See how smart Mary is? She got all the words right on her spelling test, and Johnny made an A-plus in arithmetic. Aren't they terrific?"

There is nothing wrong with the pursuit of perfection

at times. The problem is that too many of us apply perfectionism inappropriately. Perfection is necessary for some tasks such as programming a computer, watchmaking or building ships in bottles. However, perfection isn't necessary for the vast majority of things we do in life. In these cases, perfectionism hinders effectiveness and wastes time and energy. Being compulsively perfectionist about your car, your house, your desk, your clothes, your children, your spouse, your colleagues and so on is a needless waste of time. It can keep you from achieving the important goals in your life.

The life of a perfectionist is not a happy one because he is trying to accomplish the impossible dream. More often than not, the perfectionist is at odds with himself because he can never live up to his own expectations.

Many perfectionists are frustrated doers who fear making mistakes. They can't make a mistake if they don't do anything, so they don't do anything. The folly of such an attitude is best refuted by an anonymous quote I read which said, "Better to be a strong man with a weak point than to be a weak man without a strong point. A diamond with a flaw is more valuable than a brick without a flaw."

Keep Your Perspective

A good rule of thumb to remember is that most things seem more important in the present than they actually are. The immediacy of the present tends to make us nearsighted. As you encounter pressure-inducing situations, keep the concept of the magnified present in mind. Is it really do or die? Is it really the chance of a lifetime? Back off and view things from a lifetime perspective. Most of the time you will find things far less drastic than they originally appeared. Such a realization makes it easier to take things in stride.

Like everything else in life, effectiveness is largely a matter of attitude. Publius Syrus summed it up nicely:

A wise man will be the master of his mind
A fool will be its slave.

3
Conquering Time Wasters

CHAPTER 6

Putting an End to Putting It Off

*"If you want to make an easy job seem mighty hard,
just keep putting off doing it."*

—Olin Miller

Are you a procrastinator? If you answered yes, allow me to congratulate you for your honesty. To some degree, we all are. Procrastination is so universal, I hear there is now a National Procrastination Club whose members have been planning to meet for some time but haven't gotten around to it yet.

THE PRICE OF PROCRASTINATION

Several of the work tapes discussed in Chapter 1 are underlying beliefs that can cause us to procrastinate. Myths such as activity means productivity, the easy way is the best way, work is inherently unpleasant, the justice myth and the myth that we work best under pressure can give us plenty of reasons for delaying or not doing.

Procrastination is often difficult to detect because it's

a nonentity. The tasks you perform are what you get done, and the rest are left undone or postponed. However, procrastination becomes a problem when you neglect or delay doing those things that are important to you.

We pay a gigantic price for the luxury of indulging ourselves in the lap of procrastination. It's the universal effectiveness killer. Here are some ways in which "putting it off" takes its enormous toll.

Waste of the Present

Dale Carnegie wrote, "One of the most tragic things I know about human nature is that all of us tend to put off living. We are all dreaming of some magical rose garden over the horizon—instead of enjoying the roses that are blooming outside our windows today."

This is perhaps the greatest price of procrastination because today is really all we have. All the talking, hoping and wishing about the future isn't making the most of the present and it certainly isn't building for the future. The past is history and tomorrow is only a vision, but the procrastinator wastes today. Worse yet, procrastination is terribly habit-forming and we can all guess what the procrastinator is going to do when tomorrow becomes today. The cycle will repeat itself and our procrastinator is on his way to . . .

An Unfulfilled Life

A fulfilled life means accomplishment and enjoyment each day. But procrastination is an immobilizer that blocks fulfillment. To the procrastinator there is always tomorrow, so today never has to count for anything. This creates a vacuum in the present, and many less desirable things appear to fill the void.

Boredom

Laurence Peter once spoke of a teacher so boring that he could light a room by leaving. If you know any boring people (and who doesn't?), you will usually find that they themselves are bored. You may choose to pity these people, but I don't. Boredom is a way of life and a great escape for not using present moments constructively. If you want to be bored that's your choice, but you'll never convince me that life is boring. Choosing boredom as a way of life is merely another way the procrastinator structures his time.

The Anxiety of Working Under Pressure

By waiting until the last minute, the procrastinator provides himself with numerous opportunities to fill his life with anxieties. If you think such people are in short supply, go down to your local post office on the evening of April 15th and watch the traffic. If you didn't know better, you might think the government was giving away money rather than collecting it.

Impotent Goals

Many procrastinators, like doers, have goals. Of course, the procrastinator never gets around to pursuing his goals, much less achieving them. Consequently, his goals aren't really goals but rather just a lot of hot air. Such people are easily recognized by their chronic case of the "I'm gonnas."

135

- I'm gonna go to Europe.
- I'm gonna get a better job.
- I'm gonna go back to school.
- I'm gonna buy a house.
- I'm gonna quit smoking.
- I'm gonna go on a diet.
- I'm gonna be a wheel someday. (The procrastinator's theme song.)

The list could go on forever, so if you'll pardon the expression I'm gonna tell you about another high price we pay for putting things off.

The Constant Plague of Unsolved Problems

There are some problems in life that time and inaction can cure. However, the chronic procrastinator treats most if not all problems this way. Ignoring or failing to recognize and deal with most problems doesn't make them go away. Worse yet, unsolved problems live to create more problems. Fail to fix a tiny leak in your roof, and one day your whole ceiling caves in. Don't watch your weight and you blow up like a balloon with resulting health complications. Ignore doing the important but unpleasant aspects of your job and you may find yourself without one. Unsolved problems are much like vermin. If you don't make the effort to extinguish them, they can breed at an extremely high rate and compound your misery.

Continuous Frustration

Nobody likes being frustrated. Frustration is not getting what you want out of life. Who needs that?

Evidently the procrastinator must, because that's what he sets himself up for. Instead of taking action, he says to himself, "I hope," "I wish," "Maybe things will get better" and other such nonsense.

An accountant I know should win a prize for continued frustration through inaction, if they ever have one. Rufus has been working for a large company for over twenty years. He's about as dynamic as a bowl of cold grits. Rufus doesn't like his "dead-end job" as he calls it, his boss or the company. He doesn't like the city he lives in. But Rufus isn't about to do anything drastic like change jobs or move to another city. He's hoping things will change. Rufus is a bachelor who has been steadily dating the same girl for over ten years. She wants to get married. When the subject is brought up, Rufus always replies, "You know, we're just really starting to know each other. Let's give it a little more time."

A few years back I ran into Rufus and he was very frustrated and upset. He had been evicted from his apartment, where he had lived for several years. I asked him why he had been evicted and the answer was astounding. It seems Rufus didn't like taking out the garbage; consequently, he didn't. One day, the apartment manager got wind of a foul odor coming from Rufus's apartment and went in to investigate. There she found countless bags of garbage that Rufus had managed to accumulate over an extended period of time. Both Rufus and the garbage were put out in short order.

The last I heard, Rufus was in a new apartment and well on his way to building a new rubbish collection. However, I'm not really concerned about Rufus. He's going to get it all together—tomorrow—he hopes.

Other Results of Procrastination

Poor Health—Along with injury and premature death, this is another price we often pay for procrastinating. Sweeping symptoms of medical problems under the rug and putting off getting them checked can be fatal.

Driving around an extra week on bad tires or worn-out brakes is another potential disaster area spawned by procrastinating. Important things are seldom urgent, until it's too late.

A Mediocre Career—This is still another price paid for the luxury of delay. Many a procrastinator is content to stay in a lackluster position or career that he really isn't suited for. Missed business opportunities often result from procrastination. Delay calling on a customer today and your competitor will take him away from you. Delay updating your product and the competition will make you obsolete. Inaction leads to poor results, or, worse yet, no results at all.

A Life of Indecision—Every decision is an opportunity to gain some control over your future. However, when you put off decisions you are forfeiting that opportunity. Sooner or later circumstances will prevail and your right of choice will be taken away. By being indecisive you allow yourself to become a slave to your future rather than the master of it. This syndrome has ruined many managerial careers.

Poor Interpersonal Relationships—These are another consequence of leading the life of inaction. Whenever a conflict arises the procrastinator shies away from

138

further contact rather than trying to amicably resolve it with the other person. If a conflict can't be resolved, the procrastinator still does nothing. Spending your career working for a boss you dislike and staying in a bad marriage or sour relationship are all too typical of the person of inaction. In addition to the frustration of clinging to bad relationships, the procrastinator simultaneously foregoes the opportunity to form happy and meaningful relationships.

Fatigue—This should come as no surprise. Although it may look easy, procrastination is not what it seems. It's a damned excruciating way to spend your time and energy. However, in the final analysis it's the procrastinator's choice to be fatigued. He works hard all day struggling with doubt, indecision, delay, frustration and boredom. After all that, it's no wonder he's tired.

WHY WE PROCRASTINATE

With the price of procrastination so exorbitant, it is only natural to ask "Why do we do it?" Most but not all reasons for procrastinating are emotional in nature.

To Escape an Overwhelming Task

By filling up present moments with trivia, you can escape doing something that you know is important but seems too large to tackle. For example, Ben, a department manager, has the task ahead of him of preparing a semiannual status report. He looks at the job and thinks, "If I start this now, it's just going to be one damn interruption after another." So he deludes himself into believing he'll do the report someday when he won't have to worry about interruptions, and spends the rest of his day writing meaningless memos, answering the telephone, conversing with colleagues and writing routine correspondence. He goes home tired but contented. After all, he got a lot done today! As the report's deadline date approaches, Ben will embark on a crash program and probably end up writing the report at night or over the weekend, complaining the whole time about how overworked he is.

To Escape an Unpleasant Task

All of us have important but unpleasant things to do from time to time. Given the choice of doing anything pleasant rather than something unpleasant we will usually choose the former.

Take the case of poor old Charlie. His garage is wall-to-wall chaos. One Saturday morning, Charlie gets the ultimatum from his wife—clean out the garage this afternoon or sleep in it tonight. On his way out to the garage, Charlie notices that his neighbor, Fred, is having car trouble. Being a great lover of mechanics, and a good neighbor, Charlie spends the next two hours helping Fred fix his car. Then Fred has Charlie over for a beer. It's the least he can do for Charlie. Once inside, Fred and Charlie spend the next three hours absorbed in the football game on television. What a game! State's playing the number one team in the nation.

When the game comes to an end, so has Saturday afternoon. Charlie goes home to a chagrined wife who gives him a look reminiscent of the Spanish inquisition. Charlie ends up cleaning and organizing the garage that night. The darkness hinders his efforts and he does a mediocre job, which gives him another payoff.

To Excuse Poor Work

This is one of the biggest cop-outs of delay. "I just couldn't get to it until the last minute. If only I had had more time, I could have done a better job." As a college professor, I frequently hear that excuse from students who submit poorly written term papers. The most amazing part of that excuse is that term papers are assigned the first week of class and collected the last. Yet I hear that excuse at least once each semester.

To Gain Sympathy

"See how hard I try?" is the battle cry of the procrastinating warrior. The translation of such a statement is "Don't see how little I have done." Ben, looking haggard and overworked, turns in a half-baked report to his boss a week late. After stumbling around in the darkness for six hours, Charlie drags in, covered from head to toe with dirt, and flops into bed, a picture of total fatigue. Anxiety-laden students beg the professor for term-paper deadline extensions. Don't you feel sorry for all these poor, unfortunate victims of circumstance? Hogwash!

To Get Someone Else to Do the Job

There's certainly nothing wrong with delegating most tasks. However, there are easier, quicker and more direct ways to go about it than playing the put-off game with someone. Such covert behavior is a waste of everybody's time. Ideas for effectively delegating are discussed in Chapter 9.

To Protect a Weak Self-Image

An inferior self-image and the accompanying fears of failure or success are other reasons for inaction. By deluding yourself with excuses for not doing, you don't risk the anxiety and pain of failure. Simultaneously, you can avoid success and any problems that you fear may accompany it. You can just be your same old wonderful procrastinating self complete with all the accompanying miseries, misfortunes and frustrations that you have had in the past. All of which adds up to one of the biggest emotional reasons for not doing ...

To Avoid Change

You give yourself a lifetime to be a bored, critical, indecisive, unachieving, blah individual. And the best part is you get to blame your misfortunes on everything and everyone else but you. The easy-way tape plays on.

Other Reasons for Procrastination

Not all procrastination is bad and not all of the reasons we procrastinate are emotional cop-outs for inaction. There are several nonemotional reasons for procrastinating. I'll only mention them here because they have been discussed in detail previously:

1. Improper goals can be one source of delay. Are you sure this goal is still important to you or necessary? Is it really *your* goal?

2. Insufficient information can block problems from

being solved, decisions from being made and things from getting done.

3. Goals without deadlines tend never to get achieved, or get achieved much later than goals with deadlines.

4. Overcommitment inevitably leads to procrastination. Saying yes to everything decreases the chances of completing any one thing.

5. Unrealistic time estimates can cause bottlenecks and delays. Remember Murphy. Everything takes longer than you expect.

TECHNIQUES FOR CREATING MOMENTUM

When Newton formulated his law of inertia I'm sure he wasn't thinking about human behavior. However, the law applies equally well to people and objects. A body (human or otherwise) at rest tends to remain at rest and a body in motion tends to remain in motion.

When procrastinating you are at rest, and the hardest part is getting started. Once in motion most of us will tend to remain in motion. I once heard the remark that the most difficult problem in life is getting out of a warm bed into a cold room. Once you get up, the day is underway. So it is with the other tasks of life. Gain momentum, the task is well on its way to being completed.

The following is a list of ideas for creating momentum. For any given task one or more of them can help you to conquer procrastination.

1. Recognize and acknowledge the futility of procrastination as a way of living. By procrastinating, you put yourself under a useless emotional strain. Do you

really want a life of frustration, fatigue and boredom? Of course not. No one does. To the degree you let yourself live a life of delay and inaction, you invite the dark side of living into your existence. Admittedly it's often tough to get up and tackle difficult tasks, but what's your alternative? Spending your life rotting on the vine like an unpicked tomato may be your idea of living, but I seriously doubt it. You wouldn't be taking the time to read this book if you didn't value your life.

2. Break down overwhelming tasks into small tasks. Anyone who has ever performed monumental feats knows the value of this idea. Henry Ford once remarked, "Nothing is particularly hard if you divide it into small jobs." It was on this idea that the auto assembly line was founded.

Do you want to write a two-hundred-page book? Write a page each day and you will finish in less than seven months. Do you want to be a millionaire? Invest $1,000 a year starting at age thirty and get a fifteen percent compounded annual return. At age sixty-five, you will have a million.

Whenever you have a seemingly overwhelming task, divide it up into as many five- or ten-minute subtasks as you can think of. Write them down and list them in the order to be performed. Tackle the first one now. When you can spare another five or ten minutes do another, and so on. Once you get started, you'll gain the momentum to finish the job. Large successes are usually a series of small ones. "A journey of a thousand miles begins with one step."

3. Face unpleasant tasks squarely. A humorist once defined an optimist as a woman who leaves the dinner dishes because she will feel more like washing them in the

morning. Most unpleasant tasks are like the dinner dishes. Ignoring them doesn't make them disappear and usually makes things worse. Why keep clouding your horizons when a little effort will get you sunny skies?

One way to tackle an unpleasant task is to reserve a small amount of time, say ten or fifteen minutes, resolve to work on it at that time and quit when your time is up. Large problems such as preparing a budget, taking an inventory or cleaning out the attic can be handled this way.

Unfortunately, some unpleasant tasks don't lend themselves to this approach. Tasks such as firing an employee or being the bearer of bad news can't usually be handled in a piecemeal manner. In such a case, your best choice is to do it and let it be done. Not doing it today only insures that you will feel equally burdened with it and other tasks tomorrow. Realize that you are merely compounding your workload with inaction and then resolve to do the task—now.

4. Do a start-up task. Sometimes a little spontaneous physical action is all you need to get you in the mood to start a major task. Do you have a yard full of leaves to rake? Walk down to the corner store and buy some lawn leaf bags—now. Do you have a report to write? Take a piece of paper and make a list of ten major points you wish to include and rank them in the order in which you plan to discuss them—now. Have you been putting off answering a letter? Address the envelope—now. Do you need to settle a misunderstanding with a customer? Look up his telephone number—now.

5. Take advantage of your moods. How many times have you said to yourself "I'm just not in the mood"? The idea here is to use your moods to your advantage. For

145

example, you may not feel like writing that report today, but do you feel like calling someone who can give you some helpful information? You may not feel like repairing the broken TV antenna but do you feel like gathering the necessary hardware? Remember those things you have been delaying and put your moods to work for you rather than against you.

6. Think of something you have been putting off that's important. List the good things that could possibly happen by doing the task. Now list all the disadvantages that could come about as a result of inaction. You usually will find that the advantages of action far outweigh the liabilities of inaction. Such a technique helps create enthusiasm to get you going.

For example, let's suppose it's spring. You want to plant a vegetable garden in your backyard, but just can't seem to get around to it. Your list might look something like this:

ADVANTAGES OF ACTION	DISADVANTAGES OF INACTION
1. Fresh-tasting, home-grown vegetables are a real treat.	1. Time is running out. If I don't start soon, I won't get another chance for a year.
2. With the additional saving in grocery money we can afford the camping trip to Yellowstone this year.	2. Without the garden we will have to content ourselves with a lesser vacation.
3. Growing a garden is good exercise and a great diversion from my job.	3. Without some additional diversions, I'll propably spend my spare time worrying about my job.

4. This is a opportunity to learn by doing something I've never done before.

4. I'm getting a little old to believe in the Jolly Green Giant. Lonely is a man without his own niblets.

5. I can make this a family project that we can all learn, enjoy, participate and take pride in. This can bring us all closer.

5. We all seem to be drifting in separate ways. Without some common goals, family unity can be severely damaged.

7. Make a commitment to someone or a wager with someone. Tell your boss that you will have the budget prepared a week early or buy him dinner of his choice. If you are a sales representative, bet one of your colleagues (or more than one if you wish) that you will up your last month's sales by twenty percent or buy all the drinks at a future happy hour. If you bet with someone, be sure there's something in it for you if you win. You want both an incentive for reaching your goal and a penalty for falling short.

8. Give yourself a reward. This is one of my favorite methods for conquering procrastination because it's positive in nature. Find an important goal that you have been dodging and decide what would be a fitting reward for you when you achieve it. For example, you might decide to get that new briefcase you've been admiring after you add ten new customers to your list. Or how about a new pair of shoes after cleaning out the attic or shampooing the rugs? Make your reward system commensurate with the size of the task. For example, if you have been going to school at night to secure an advanced degree, promise yourself something really nice like a two-week cruise after graduation.

Besides being a lot of fun, setting up your own

reward system can be a very effective way of cutting down on procrastination. Just be honest with yourself. If you do the task be sure to give yourself the reward, and if you don't complete the task don't give yourself the reward.

9. For rational delays, the following previously discussed methods will help:

- Give yourself deadlines.
- Get more imformation.
- Avoid overcommitment.
- Set realistic time schedules.

10. Resolve to make every day count. Your life is too short to waste on inaction. George Allen said it best when he remarked, "The future is now." After living for some time with an incurable cancer, Senator Hubert Humphrey said, "You learn to treat each day as a gift." Resolve to do two things with each day before you arise in the morning: Enjoy today, and do something that will make for a better tomorrow. Every day is a treasure. Treat it as such and you will take a large step toward ending procrastination.

11. Be decisive and have the courage to act. A good working definition of courage is the ability to act when you are afraid.

Take the case of Alfred. Alfred was a fifty-year-old chief engineer with a wife and family. Since age forty, Alfred had been planning to open his own manufacturing concern. He had a product, a good market, technical expertise, capital and potential customers lined up. However, Alfred just wouldn't make that final commitment to open his own business. He was overwhelmed by a case of the "what ifs": "What if the whole thing goes belly up?" "What if I can't send the kids to college?" "What if I can't pay the mortgage?" and so on. Alfred was being held back by fear and, as Lloyd Douglas wrote, "If a man harbors any sort of fear, it . . . makes him landlord to a ghost."

With the encouragement of his wife and children, Alfred made the big move and opened his own business, where he has been very successful both personally and financially. I spoke with him one day after he had been in business about five years. His only regrets were the years of enjoyment and satisfaction he had missed by not going into business earlier. His thoughts reminded me of Maurice Freehill's question: "Who is more foolish, the child afraid of the dark or the man afraid of the light?"

By delaying action, you waste valuable time and, as Alfred found out, all the money in the world cannot buy back one moment (much less years) of lost time. It's gone forever.

Remember, you're better than you think and can take much more adversity than you ever dreamed of. Cure yourself of self-defeating statements as "I'm gonna," "I wish," "I want," "I hope" and so on. Make something happen! Your actions will speak for themselves.

12. Refuse to be bored. Are you living in a rut? Get out of it. Drive another route to work. Eat lunch at a different restaurant. Change your hairstyle or buy some new clothes. Find an exotic food you're afraid of and purposely order or cook some. Replace the familiar with the unfamiliar. As Auntie Mame said, "Life is a banquet." So why sit in a corner each day with a can of sardines? There's so much world and so little time.

13. Practice doing absolutely nothing. When you find you are avoiding an important task, go sit in a chair and see how long you can go without doing anything.

You will probably find yourself rather eager to get moving in a matter of minutes. Most of us are rather poor at the art of doing nothing. When you can no longer stand the interlude of nothingness, resolve to tackle that job you've been avoiding, and begin it—now.

14. Frequently ask yourself, "What's the best use of my time and energy right now?" If the answer is not what you are doing at the moment, stop that and put your time and energy to work on a more important task.

15. Finally, ask yourself this question each morning: "What is the greatest problem facing me and what am I going to do about it *today?*"

CHAPTER 7

Minimizing Those Costly Interruptions

*"A committee is a group of men who individually
can do nothing but collectively can meet and
decide that nothing can be done."*

—*Alfred E. Smith*

"Of course I'll serve on the committee. You can always count on me."

"My door is always open."

"I'm as close as your telephone whenever you need me."

What the above three statements have in common is that they each can be translated into a fourth: "I'd love to waste my time. When do we start?"

What's that? You disagree? You say you are paid to do these things? If you are being rewarded for being available rather than being effective, then your organization's priorities are not results-oriented. Unfortunately, the growth of massive bureaucracies is providing more jobs with a lesser premium on results. Activities, rituals, pastimes and meaningless red tape have become the yardsticks for performance.

Nevertheless, productive people want to produce and it offends the very essence of their being to do otherwise. Are you someone who abhors committee meetings and has an equally strong distaste for being continuously on tap for random telephone calls and drop-in visitors? If so, God bless you. You have a basic predisposition toward effectiveness. Given half an opportunity you will likely work less, accomplish more and do something meaningful with your life.

Meetings, visitors and telephone calls are not necessarily unproductive any more than gunpowder is a necessarily destructive substance. It's all a matter of application. Unfortunately, the seeming legitimacy of these common time wasters allows them to proliferate unchecked. If we take steps to make judicious use of meetings, visitors and the telephone, these time wasters can become tools to aid effectiveness. Let's consider them one at a time.

WHY WE HAVE SO MANY USELESS MEETINGS

When it comes to meetings most of us behave as though we had never heard that time is money. Meetings are terribly expensive and most of us believe that this is the number one time waster. How much does a meeting cost? Calculate the per-hour salaries of those on a committee and add them up. It's very common to have meetings that cost thousands of dollars per hour. However, most of us don't tend to think of meetings in dollars and cents. Consequently, one reason for so many useless meetings is that we fail to recognize the cost. Other popular reasons for holding meetings follow.

To Provide an Audience for Someone

Some people like to hear themselves talk so much that they just have to share it with a group. The late Senator Everett Dirksen was delivering a lengthy discourse at a Senate committee meeting. After being interrupted several times by a colleague, Dirksen turned to the interrupter and said, "My dear sir, you are interrupting the man I most want to hear."

How many meetings have you been to where all you did was listen to someone's views on everything from world economics to the mating of Great Danes with Chihuahuas? Far too many, I'm sure. It's a very expensive ego trip, but one reason that we have so many useless meetings.

To Socialize

There are very few of us who can tolerate working alone for extended periods of time. Meetings provide a great excuse for us to get together and quell any pangs of loneliness we feel. In addition to conducting business, Ralph can talk to Bill about his golf game and George can flirt with the boss's secretary who takes the minutes. Everyone would be better off if they just threw a party, but that's only for special occasions. We can't afford to admit to ourselves that we aren't getting anything done, so we meet and socialize under the guise of committee work.

To Escape from Being Effective

Meetings are an excuse for poor work or no work at all. You can volunteer for many committees and fill up

153

virtually all your time serving on them. This gives you a perfect excuse for ignoring the most important aspects of your job. Better yet, you can dodge unpleasant tasks or turn in assignments late and say you were too busy to get around to them last week because your time was taken up in meetings. Since meetings are an acceptable way to structure work time, you appear to be an ambitious, caring soul with many irons in the fire. The fact that your time would have been better spent vacationing in the Caribbean is of no consequence. The activity myth strikes again.

Habit

The only real reason for having many meetings is that it's always been that way. Regularly scheduled meetings are often prime candidates for wasting time.

People are usually resistant to change. As a result, traditions tend to live on long after their purpose has passed away. Some years back I read that the federal government had a board of teatasters whose sole purpose was to taste tea. The board was considered by many to be a waste of taxpayers' money. However, it had been in existence since the eighteenth century and had managed to survive for some two hundred years mainly on the basis of tradition. At the time I read the article the government was considering disbanding the board, but I really don't know if it did.

To Pass the Buck

Very often a decision can and should be made by an individual but he is reluctant to do so. As a result he forms a committee and asks them for a decision or a recommendation which he automatically adopts. If the decision meets with an ill fate, the buck can be passed to the committee and no one person is held responsible. Such a strategy is frequently utilized by members of the C.Y.A. (short for "cover your ass"). As Richard Buskirk wrote, "Something that is everyone's responsibility is no one's responsibility. . . . Is it any wonder that educational institutions are so ineptly managed? The places are largely run by committees."

Of course, the individual who delegates decisions to a committee isn't in actuality avoiding responsibility. He still is accountable for the decision, so he only fools himself if he delegates, thinking he's passing the buck.

To Fool People into Believing They Are Participating in Important Decisions

Please don't misunderstand me. Many committees do make use of the capabilities of people to make important decisions. However, all too often the boss forms a committee to make recommendations and then does whatever the hell he wants or, worse yet, tells the committee what kind of recommendation he wants. The meetings are usually held in the spirit of "All in favor say 'aye,' all opposed say 'fired.' " Such pseudo-participation is only a useless waste of everyone's time. Why ask for advice if your mind is made up?

When Richard Nixon was President, members of Congress accused him of pseudo-participation. Legislators accused him of fleeing to Camp David, Key Biscayne or San Clemente to make decisions and then inviting them to the Oval Office to see what they thought of his decisions.

GETTING THE MOST FROM MEETINGS

Hendrik van Loon once defined a committee as "a group which succeeds in getting something done only when it consists of three members, one of whom happens to be sick and another absent." Fortunately, it doesn't have to be that way. With a little forethought and diligence we can eliminate many useless meetings and make the remaining ones more effective. The following ideas are presented with those purposes in mind.

General Guidelines

1. Begin by taking an inventory of all existing committees and meetings held. Write down the purpose of each. Are they really necessary? Have some outlived their usefulness? Can any be consolidated or eliminated? If so, do it.

2. Have a minimum number of standing committees. No committee should be allowed to linger on indefinitely. Regularly question the purpose of each committee's existence.

3. Every time you form a committee, state its purpose, give it a deadline for achieving its purpose, if possible, and dissolve it when it has achieved its goal.

4. Never call a meeting when there is a reasonable alternative. Can a conference call be arranged instead? Can the job be done by an individual?

5. Never go to a meeting if you can send someone else.

6. Keep the number of members attending as small as possible. Large committees get very cumbersome and usually end up being dominated by a small number of people.

156

Preparation

Working smart in meetings is much like the rest of life—an investment of time and energy in forethought and planning pays handsome dividends.

1. If you decide to call a meeting, pin down precisely what you expect to accomplish at the meeting. Every meeting should have at least one goal and, if there is more than one goal, a set of priorities.

2. Set a starting and ending time for each meeting and resolve to stick to them. If people arrive late, begin without them. With respect to scheduling, it's a good idea to schedule meetings back to back, before lunch or near the end of the day. Such a practice often prevents long, drawn-out meetings.

3. Make an agenda and circulate it well in advance to those who will be attending. On the agenda list the goals, topics to be covered and time of beginning and ending. It also helps to provide participants with background reading material prior to the meeting so they can be prepared to discuss the issues without wasting meeting time.

4. Tool up for meetings. Prepare exhibits that help clarify or illustrate points you wish to make. Charts, graphs, handouts, slides and chalkboards can all be helpful. Provide note pads and pencils for participants. Check out the physical surroundings for comfort, size, lighting and ventilation.

Execution

Many meetings only result in calling another. The following guidelines can help prevent your best-laid plans from going up in smoke at the conference.

1. Stick to the agenda that has been prepared and stay on course. Focus on the purpose of the meeting and the topic that has the floor at the moment. Too many meetings easily get sidetracked or degenerate into bull sessions. It's the responsibility of the chairman to prevent this from happening.

Another related problem is that some people like to complicate issues and problems during meetings. I have seen a motion get amended so many times that participants don't know what they're voting on. Try to handle issues singly and discourage ambiguous and trivial complications.

2. If you are invited to attend a meeting and feel you have nothing to contribute, don't go. If you can't get out of it, bring something else to do at the meeting. Meetings can command the presence of your body but they will only waste your time if you allow them to. Catch up on your reading or write letters if it's a large meeting. If the meeting is one at which you have to look as if you're paying attention, you can play the role, look intelligent and fantasize, conjure up fond memories or consider some important decisions. No one will ever know the difference. Remember the Rule of the Great: When somebody you greatly admire and respect appears to be thinking deep thoughts he is probably thinking about lunch.

3. If you are conducting a meeting, excuse those who have finished making their contribution before the meeting is over. If you are attending and have made your contribution, ask to be excused.

4. If you're chairing a meeting, it's your responsibility to try and involve everyone in the discussion. If some

people are reluctant to speak, ask them for an opinion. Usually, however, the problem is someone who talks too much and often gets sidetracked. If this is the case calmly keep discussing the issue at hand and stick with your agenda.

If you find people are bored or bogged down with the issue at hand, tactical sidetracking can sometimes get things going. The idea here is to get off the track completely, but the purpose is to get people to open up. Once they seem to be more receptive and enthusiastic, go back to the agenda.

5. Sometimes meetings drag on because people are just too comfortable to get up. If so, consider holding a stand-up meeting. It's amazing how quickly things can get done when people aren't sitting around on their duffs. As a more subtle alternative you might consider using less comfortable chairs. Using uncomfortable chairs is an old trick employed by some restaurants to prevent customers from tying up tables for hours. Perhaps this strategy can prevent meetings from dragging on as well.

Follow-up

1. Have someone present to take accurate and relevant minutes at the meetings. It is best if this isn't one of the participants but rather a third party such as a secretary. The minutes should be recorded, duplicated and sent to all participants as soon as possible. After a few days most of us remember only a small fraction of what transpired at a meeting. A good recording system is essential.

2. Prepare a checklist before each meeting stating

what you want to accomplish. At the end of the meeting, compare the results with original agenda. This can serve as a bench mark for measuring the effectiveness of meetings.

In summary, the effectiveness of meetings is best enhanced by eliminating and avoiding the useless ones. Practically every organization has its share of meetings, some of which should be avoided like the plague. Assuming certain meetings are necessary, they should focus on goals, and their contribution to goals should be regularly measured.

LIFE WITH DROP-INS

One of the chief problems of the work world is drop-ins—drop-in visitors. It's quite common for many of us to spend one-half or more of our workday dealing with the unexpected interruptions of the visitor. Others of us make our livings by playing the role of a visitor. If you are a sales rep, such is the nature of your job.

Like meetings, drop-in visitors give us all sorts of excuses to be ineffective. We can socialize, provide an audience, ask others for their ideas (when our mind is usually made up anyway) and practice the art of procrastination with all of its wonderful payoffs.

Of course, visitors are necessary. Many of them keep us informed and provide us with ideas that enable us to be more effective. My recommendation is that you minimize the unnecessary ones and schedule necessary visits so that they don't cause random havoc on your workday. With that basic policy in mind, here are Thirteen Ways to Manage Drop-in Visits:

1. Pin down who your main drop-ins are. Keep a

160

visitor log for a week or two, and write down who each visitor is and how much of your time he takes. Usually you will find the 80/20 rule holds true: Eighty percent of your time spent in visits will be taken up by twenty percent, or less, of your drop-in visitors. Once you know who your main interrupters are, you will be better able to devise a strategy for accommodating and/or minimizing their visits.

2. Close your door. This can be a particular problem if you are in a supervisory or managerial position. Leadership and supervisory training programs stress the importance of managers being available to confer with subordinates. However, an open-door policy was never to be construed as managers always having to drop whatever they're doing to entertain a visitor. Being accessible is important, but always being accessible is a blueprint for wasting time.

An open door invites the person roaming the halls to come in and waste your time. If you can't understand why you have to work such long hours, try closing your door for a good part of your day. It works wonders.

3. Remove excess chairs and other social amenities from your office. If your office contains a number of chairs or if it's equipped with a coffeepot, you may be playing the role of informal host in your job. People will think of your place as the local gathering spot for good times and bull sessions. While it's important to be sociable, you are probably being paid to do a good deal more than that. If you are playing host and are still on top of things, there's no cause for alarm. However, if you love to socialize and you find yourself falling behind, inform your friends of the problem and remove the social amenities from your office. If they are really your friends, they will

understand. If someone complains, offer to move the chairs and the coffeepot to his office.

4. If someone wants to talk with you, volunteer to go to his office to chat. Such a practice gives you control over the time of the visit. As soon as business is transacted, you can get up and go back to your empty office. A drop-in visitor can't tie up your time if he doesn't get the chance to drop in.

5. If someone unexpectedly walks into your office, stand up and confer with him while standing. Such body language usually indicates to the other party that you're busy and have more pressing things to do. Allowing drop-ins to sit down only increases the odds of their staying too long.

6. Rearrange your desk and chair so that you aren't facing the door. If your door is open but your back is to it, the hall socialities will be less likely to drop in.

7. If someone knocks on your door, confer with him in the hall. Once again, the idea is to keep visitors from firmly planting themselves in your office.

8. Position your secretary's desk where he or she can screen your unexpected visitors. A good secretary can handle many routine questions and problems and greatly reduce your time spent with drop-ins.

9. Schedule visiting hours and see visitors only at those times, unless there is an emergency. Your secretary can schedule appointments for visitors and inform you about the nature and purpose of their visit.

10. Be candid with visitors. If someone drops in and asks if you're busy, answer "Yes." If you can see them for only five minutes, tell them so. If they need to see you for further discussion, arrange for an appointment during visiting hours.

11. Once a visitor is in your office you can control the length of the visit several ways. If you feel a visitor has transacted his business and is overstaying, simply be quiet. Don't contribute to a needless conversation and there won't be one. Another way is to ask your secretary, prior to the visit, to interrupt you—buzz you or walk in and remind you of that meeting or next appointment (real or imagined)—after the visitor has been there for a specified period of time. Of course, you can simply say you have to be at a meeting in ten minutes and bring the visit to a close.

12. Build time into your schedule to allow for unexpected visitors. No matter how much you plan, scheme and screen visitors, some will inevitably get through. Keeping a loose schedule, as was previously mentioned, is the best way to prevent the unexpected from hindering your effectiveness.

13. Use your coffee breaks or lunch hours to meet with visitors. Many visitors have important and necessary reasons for conferring with you. Meeting these people for midmorning breaks or luncheons makes multiple use of time. Many high-level executives schedule regular luncheons with their assistants or colleagues for the purpose of exchanging information. It's an idea all of us can use if we are plagued with an overabundance of visitors.

MAKING THE TELEPHONE WORK FOR YOU

Do you suffer from telephonitis? Most of us do. It's a disease of epidemic proportions that can lead to gigantic wastes of time, energy and money. More often than not the disease isn't contagious and is caused by curiosity and a lack of self-discipline on the part of the victim.

It's always great fun to be interrupted from the task at hand by the ringing or buzzing of the telephone. Who could it be? What do they want? The mystery of the unknown is always more appealing than attending to the task at hand. So we take the calls as they come and allow our work to be randomly disrupted.

Actually, telephonitis is the result of a good thing put to misuse. The following ideas can help you in the prevention and cure of this dreadful effectiveness killer.

1. Log your calls for one week. Write down who calls, when they call, what they want and the length of time on the telephone. Log your outgoing calls in a similar manner. The 80/20 rule will probably apply— eighty percent of your calls come from less than twenty percent of all callers. After you have completed a week's log, answer the following questions:

- Who called?
- Whom did you call?
- Which calls were important?
- How many calls could be handled by someone else?
- How much time was spent on unnecessary calls?

2. Make your telephone a time- and energy-saver. That's why it's there. The telephone is a terrific labor-saving tool. You can use it for conference calls rather than taking the time and expense of a meeting. You can use the telephone instead of writing letters. Costs of clerical help are increasing while the cost of long-distance calls is decreasing. The telephone gets you information in minutes that a letter could take weeks or months to acquire. Finally, you can use the telephone to save time and

164

expense of trips. Proper use of the telephone is one of our greatest effectiveness tools.

3. Establish a period of time each day for placing and receiving telephone calls. For most of us, the best time is in the morning. People are most likely to be at their offices then. Encourage your regular callers to call at those hours.

4. Have your secretary screen your calls. This can be done tactfully without making you seem inaccessible. Your secretary can say to the party, "He's rather tied up at the moment. Would you like me to interrupt him or may I have him call you back?" Most will opt for the call back.

Your secretary can also provide information to callers on routine matters, thus eliminating your need to call back.

5. Outline your information before placing outgoing calls. This will clarify the main points in your mind and you will be less likely to forget to discuss one of your reasons for calling.

6. Buy a small, three-minute hourglass and put it by your phone. Every time you get a call or make one, see if you can successfully complete it in three minutes. Don't rush, but keep a score card and see if you can reduce your telephone time each week. Make a game out of it and reward yourself each week you reduce your telephone time.

7. When you place a call set the tone of the conversation at the outset. Ask to speak to the party and tell them who is calling. Once you get your party on the line, minimize the small talk and get right to "The reason I am calling you . . ."

8. If you take the time to place or take a call, give

the other person your undivided attention. Don't shuffle papers, speak to others around you or allow yourself to be distracted. You can do only one thing well at a time. If you are interrupted, ask the other party if they would like to hold or if you can call them back. To keep others unnecessarily waiting is an inconsiderate waste of their time. They're busy too and your lack of consideration could alienate them.

9. Once you have transacted business, bring the conversation to a polite and prompt close. If you get a long-winded caller, tell him you have a pressing appointment. If that doesn't work, hang up while *you* are talking. It's not polite to hang up while he is talking but it's socially acceptable to push the button while you are. If he has anything important to say, he will call back. If not, he will probably go bother someone else.

10. Get a telephone answering machine. This is a terrific screening device for home or office. In the last several years, several makes of answering machines have come on the market at prices within the reach of practically everyone. In addition to screening calls, they answer your telephone when you can't and you never miss a call. If someone wants to get you, they leave a recorded message on the machine and calls are taken without interrupting you from whatever you have to do. Most models also have an optional attachment that plays back your messages to you if you call your machine while away from home or office.

One final thought about interruptions. You can't be interrupted if you can't be found. Therefore . . .

GET YOURSELF A HIDEAWAY

When you have important tasks to do and find yourself in dire need of solitude, its comforting to know that there is somewhere you can readily have it. Tell only those who need to know where you are going, and proceed to hibernate.

Hideaways can come in various shapes and sizes, depending on your purpose and the amount of time you need there. The following are some possible avenues you can consider to temporarily escape all interruptions:

1. Your company may have rooms set aside to provide solitude for people who need to work undisturbed.

2. Libraries are readily available places for solitude. In many of them you can rent a soundproof carrel where you are free to work undisturbed.

3. Arrange to swap offices with someone who works for another company. Such an arrangement can be beneficial to both parties if they have a frequent need for solitude.

4. You can escape to a hotel or motel—the farther away the better. Try to go where no one knows you.

5. Renting an apartment is an excellent idea if you need a great deal of uninterrupted solitude. I know a professor who does this. As a result, he has written several best-selling textbooks and made himself a small fortune. He rents an efficiency apartment where the other tenants in the complex spend their days at work. The professor works on the books in the morning when the complex is like a tomb. His afternoons are spent teaching and seeing students, and he leaves the evenings free to enjoy his family.

167

6. You can always use your car as a temporary hideaway. Drive to a secluded spot and do your working or thinking in your car.This option is often overlooked.

The point is that there are many avenues to escaping interruptions and keeping them from disrupting your life. With a little thought and imagination you can discover those that will work for you.

CHAPTER 8

Melting the
Paper Blizzard

*"Xerox: A trademark for a photocopying device
that can make rapid reproductions
of human error, perfectly."*

—Merle L. Meacham

During his career at NASA, Wernher von Braun remarked, "We can lick gravity, but sometimes the paperwork is overwhelming." Stop and think about how paper has woven itself into the very fabric of our lives. We wake up to the morning paper and for most of us, paper is to our occupations what bread is to our diets—a fattening staple. It is estimated that in 1977 there were 2.5 times more clerical employees in business than there were producers of goods and services.

Just as time is money, paper is money. Let's suppose you own a small business whose rate of profit on sales is ten percent. Your paper workload has increased and you have to hire another clerk at a salary of $150 per week, or $7,800 per year. To pay the salary of that clerk you now have to increase your yearly sales revenue by $78,000! And that's not including fringe benefits. Starting to get the picture? On the other hand, $7,800 saved is $7,800 earned and is a direct addition to profit.

Worse than the monetary costs are the needless wastes of time and energy created by the overabundant use of paper. It takes time to fill out forms, write memos, read computer printouts, prepare budgets, write reports, make fourteen copies on the copy machine and read junk mail.

CAUSES OF THE PAPER BLIZZARD

Rare indeed is the employed man or woman who doesn't feel somewhat affected by the paper blizzard. We all agree that there's too darn much. If no one seems to like all this paper it's only logical to ask, "Why is there so much paper?"

The Growth of Government

This is perhaps the greatest contributor to the paper blizzard. American institutions pay $40 billion a year just to fill out forms and reports for Uncle Sam. And the cost is increasing every year. The chairman of one large pharmaceutical manufacturer claims his company spends more manhours filling out government forms or reports than on research for cancer and heart disease combined. The chairman of a major oil refinery claims the manhours spent by his company tending to Uncle's paper work would more than adequately staff and run one of their major refineries. A major university spends $300,000 each year for personnel to fill out reports on government grants and contracts. It's been estimated that paper work adds $50 to $75 to the price of each new car. The increased entry of the government into the health care field has deluged hospitals, physicians and clinics with additional paper work. All of which costs money and will not give one iota of better care to a single patient.

Unfortunately, where there is government there is paper. And since we have so much government, this is one major reason for so much paper.

The General Information Explosion

If there is a biggest industry in our society, it has to be the knowledge industry. Broadly defined, the knowledge industry covers all of the educational institutions, the major media and any public or private institution that in some way contributes to the knowledge of humankind. Our knowledge has been increasing at an incredible rate. An engineer or scientist who doesn't keep up with the state of the art is obsolete in less than five years. Much the same holds true for many other technical and non-technical fields. Each year, approximately thirty-five thousand new book titles are published by about thirteen hundred publishers in the United States. Add to this the countless number of newspapers, journals, pamphlets and so on, and you have another major contributor to the paper blizzard.

Copy Machines

These are another major contributor to the paper blizzard. Practically every office has some type of copy machine, be it photocopy, ditto, mimeograph or whatever. If you're going to run five copies, why not run seven or eight? Who knows—you may need those extra few. It's that type of thinking that causes our effectiveness to drown in our own clutter.

Insecurity

Once again, it's our old work myth: If you create a lot of paper work for yourself and others, then everyone gets to keep busy and no one has to feel guilty about not having enough work to do. Busy hands are happy hands. An idle mind is the devil's workshop. Just keep shuffling those papers.

We Don't Trust Each Other

Everybody wants everything in writing. The popular notion in todays society is "Don't trust nobody." Perhaps with good cause we have adopted mistrust as a common societal value. However, the fact is that if more than a small percentage of us were totally untrustworthy, the very foundations of our society would shake. We may not realize it but we are all highly dependent on each other.

Somehow we feel much safer if things are in writing. This feeling has been so magnified that we spend much of our time documenting and verifying details of little or no consequence, and seeing to it that everyone gets a copy.

The Growth of Computers

Along with EDP (electronic data pollution) the growing use of computers has been another great culprit involved in the proliferation of paper. Some computers print out at the rate of thousands of lines per minute, making it very easy for computers to turn out reams of useless data reports as well as numerous pieces of junk mail and meaningless documents.

HOW TO MELT THE BLIZZARD

The chances of any one person melting the paper blizzard are much like the chances of melting an iceberg with a match. The growth of government, computers, copy machines and knowledge has gathered such momentum that you can almost certainly count on having to contend with even more paper in the future. However, this doesn't prevent you from taking a number of positive steps to protect yourself from the storm. The following ideas will require awareness, recognition and change with respect to how you deal with paper. Paper use, like time use, is mainly habit and many habits are effectiveness killers. Melting the paper blizzard, like charity, starts at home and begins with getting your own house in order.

If You Don't Like the Paper Blizzard, Don't Contribute to It

You wouldn't declare war on your worst enemy and then provide him with ammunition. Take a similar approach with unnecessary paper. Declare war on it and make your first strategy to generate as little paper as possible.

1. Begin by focusing on the results you hope to achieve. Your purpose to get results, not shuffle paper. If picking up a piece of paper and acting on it furthers your achievement, go ahead and take care of it. If not, put it aside or, better yet, throw it away. Such an approach will find you eliminating a good amount of unnecessary paper.

2. Put only the bare necessities in writing. Why send out memos when face-to-face communication will get your meaning across better? Whenever you are tempted to document something ask yourself, "What's the worst that can happen by not recording this?" If the answer isn't too bad, don't record it. All too often information that we document is being documented in other places as well. A great deal of unnecessary paper is the result of needless duplication. If someone writes you a letter requesting information, answer it on their letter. This will cut your clerical expense as well as correspondence time.

3. Screen yourself from unnecessary paper. Prepare a priority list of paper work that you should handle and have your secretary handle the routine paper chores, sort out paper that needs your attention and rank items in order of importance. Take your name off of unnecessary reading lists, mailing and subscription lists.

4. Don't be a "copycat." Copy machines hinder our effectiveness although they are designed to do the opposite. Every time you're tempted to make that extra copy, remember the excess baggage that you're creating for yourself and others.

5. "If in doubt, throw it out." That was the motto of Marks & Spencer, a large British retail chain who declared war on paper. Deciding that paper work was becoming cost-prohibitive, they launched a campaign to simplify, eliminate and throw away unnecessary paper. Store managers were given more trust and fewer procedures to adhere to. Company financial reporting was less concerned with perfectionist to-the-penny accounting and more with reasonable approximations. Within two years, Marks & Spencer did away with twenty-two million forms weighing

one hundred five tons. Morale, profits and productivity all increased.

Never understimate the value of a wastebasket. It's rapidly becoming more and more necessary for success in any endeavor. Go through your files twice a year and throw out the unessential, outdated items. Don't file or keep any piece of paper unless you think it's absolutely necessary.

6. "Try to handle each piece of paper only once" is one of Alan Lakein's best rules for melting the paper blizzard. If you pick up a piece of paper, don't put it down without doing something that will help move it on its way. If you can throw it away, that's the best alternative. If it needs a reply, answer it. The main idea is to do something, no matter how small, to get the paper behind you. Every time you pick up a piece of paper needing your action, failing to act only means you'll have to double your time and energy spent on it by picking it up again.

If you find yourself shuffling the same piece of paper, put a dot on it every time you pick it up. As the dots start to accumulate you will be reminded to move the paper on its way before it looks like it has the measles.

7. Use the telephone. Many of us grew up in another era when the cost of communicating via long-distance telephone calls was not cost justifiable. Today things are quite different, but many of us are unaware of or refuse to recognize that fact. A long-distance call, in addition to eliminating paper, saves time by getting an instant response. In addition, you can ask questions or paraphrase the other party to insure that you understand him or her.

8. Master the art of dictating. Many effective people keep on top of their written correspondence through the use of a portable dictating machine. Letters can be transcribed about five times faster than they can be written out in long-hand. Additionally, this can be done while waiting for appointments, traveling to and from work or whatever. Previously unproductive minutes can become almost effortlessly productive.

If you have trouble dictating your thoughts, keep your sentences and paragraphs short. Another alternative is to record a description of what you want to say and have your secretary compose a letter from your description.

If your work entails a great deal of correspondence, I highly recommend a dictating machine, even if it means purchasing it at your own expense. It's an investment in your future aimed at increasing your effectiveness. If you aren't willing to invest in yourself, why should anyone else? In the final analysis, every person is in business for himself.

9. Start a war on paper in your office. Talk it up with your boss, your subordinates and your colleagues. They are probably as fed up with the paper blizzard as you are. People in your office can create a list of ways to cut down on the creation of needless paper. Have a "throwing out" contest. Give the person who throws out the most paper a free lunch. Provide an incentive for not using the copy machine to excess. Recognize and reward someone who comes up with a new idea for significantly saving paper. Remember, paper is money. Lee Grossman, a management consultant whose speciality is paper-work problems, believes that costs could be cut by twenty percent if paper shuffling were brought under control. Cut-

ting any company's costs by twenty percent would really light up the financial scoreboard.

Those are some of the things you can do to cut down on your active participation in the paper blizzard. Many paperwork tasks are completely unnecessary, and how effectively we handle them brings us back to the basics of writing and reading. A few words about each is in order.

How to Write Less and Communicate More

Many of us passionately hate to write anything, be it a memo, letter or report. One reason for this is that so many of us simply are poor writers. It doesn't have to be that way and the problem can usually be corrected with a little patience and practice.

"So what makes a poor writer?" you ask. In my opinion a poor writer is one who cannot or will not make himself be easily understood. There are several main reasons why poor writing abounds.

First, we inherited a great many poor writing practices from our ancestors of the nineteenth century. Flowery, verbose, bombastic language was a symbol of literacy and culture. To say "Jack propelled the prolate spheroid" was judged superior to saying "Jack threw the football." Much of our training in schools at all levels encourages us to use long words and flowery phrases when simplicity would communicate better. There's still a lot of leftover nineteenth-century baggage hanging around the ivory towers. The twentieth century is a very different era, characterized by rapid change and great scientific and technical complexity. Things are tough enough to understand without hiding them in a cloud of syllables.

Another reason we have poor writing is the need to impress each other with our vocabularies. In reading academic papers and articles, I never cease to be amazed at the attempts to make simple, obvious concepts seem deep, mystical and hard to understand.

Disorganized thinking is another cause of poor writing. Inasmuch as writing is nothing more than an expression of thought, confused thinking leads to confused writing. Related to this is the attempt to hide ignorance or poor solutions to problems in an entanglement of verbiage. Smoke-screening your thoughts will fool only the most gullible of readers. The others may not understand you, but most of them will realize that you don't want them to.

Improving your writing is much like learning to swim or play golf in that you learn by doing. Writing to communicate also involves intelligence, common sense and abandoning any childhood tapes you may be clinging to telling you what a poor writer you are. The ground rules are simple and straightforward. Here they are:

1. Get organized. What are you writing? A letter? A report? A memo? Who is it for? What is the central point you are trying to communicate? What other points do you wish to make? Do they relate to the main point? If so, how?

If you have to write something lengthy, time spent in planning and writing an outline is a tremendous time- and energy-saver. Gathering and organizing your facts before you begin to write makes for much smoother writing.

2. Once you settle down to the job of writing, use plenty of paper. Double- or triple-space lines. This way you can make revisions on your first draft without having to rewrite the entire thing(unless you deem it necessary).

In the long run you save time, energy and paper. Giving yourself plenty of writing room also gives you a feeling of greater freedom, allowing your thoughts to flow uninhibited. Be sure to choose a pen that feels comfortable. Better yet, compose at the typewriter if you can. (I personally find it difficult to type and compose simultaneously. As Woody Allen said, "I have poor interpersonal relationships with machines.")

3. Keep your reader in focus. What information do you wish to convey to him? What's the best approach for reaching him? Speak to him in his language. Tell him your central purpose at the beginning, and if it's a lengthy report, tell him how it's organized.

4. Omit needless words. In *The Elements of Style*,* by Strunk and White, one of my favorite passages about writing appears:

> Vigorous writing is concise. A sentence should contain no unnecessary words, a paragraph no unnecessary sentences, for the same reason that a drawing should have no unnecessary lines and a machine no unnecessary parts. This requires not that the writer make all his sentences short, or that he avoid all detail and treat his subjects in outline, but that every word tell.

Trimming the excess fat from your writing allows the key points to stand out by themslves. As William Haney wrote:

> ... we are reminded that the *Lord's Prayer*, the *Gettysburg Address*, the *Declaration of Independence*, and a recent government directive on cabbage prices required 56, 266, 300, and 26,911 words, respectively. Certainly it is possible to overcommunicate.

*William Strunk, Jr., and E. B. White, *The Elements of Style*, 2nd ed. (New York: Macmillan, 1972), p. 17.

After writing a letter or report always look for needless words and sentences to omit. It will do wonders for your style.

5. Keep it simple. Write to express rather than impress. Use short sentences, paragraphs and words. Try to keep your sentence lengths under twenty words and paragraphs under one hundred words. Double talk may have gotten you good grades in high-school English but it isn't the best way to clearly communicate. As Theodore Roosevelt remarked, "Writings are useless unless they are read and they cannot be read unless they are readable."

Each sentence should contain one thought and each paragraph should be built around a topic sentence that expresses the overall thought of the paragraph. Usually, though not always, the first sentence is the topic sentence.

6. Avoid ambiguous words. Certainly all words are to some degree ambiguous. However, some are more so than others. Writing is one-way communication where the reader isn't always present to ask the writer to clarify what he means.

When I was in the process of finishing graduate school and looking for a job, I received a most interesting letter from a professor at a major university. He had seen my resumé and the purpose of his letter was to ask if I was interested in considering a position at this university. In his letter, the following sentence appeared: "Living costs in this area are commensurate with other areas of the country and out housing costs are the same." How's that for ambiguity? Later on I found out that this same professor was a very successful textbook author in (you guessed it) business-letter writing!

7. Back up your general thoughts with specific facts,

ideas or illustrations. The best writing is that which is specific and definite enough to hold the reader's interest. Good writing brings pictures to the reader's mind by presenting definite illustrations.

8. Write in a style that is natural to you. Writing is nothing more than projecting your thoughts on paper. Write the way you speak and your message will more frequently come across. Don't write "The boss was subsequently terminated from his position." Write "The boss was fired." Don't write "I have found osculatory experiences to be a most pleasurable sensation." Write "I like kissing." When we write as we speak, our style tends to be vigorous, crisp and active.

9. Never underestimate your reader's intelligence or overestimate his knowledge. It's one thing to write in a simple, direct style and another to write down to your reader. Writing down, by obvious overexplanations, is an insult to the reader's intelligence and can only hurt you.

Volumes have been written on the subject of writing and I suggest you seek one of those for more information. Improving your writing effectiveness involves organization, simplification and practice.

Improving Your Reading Effectiveness

The printed word is here to stay and getting stronger every day. We hear a lot about how Johnny can't read anymore because he watches television rather than reading *Tom Sawyer*. But if Johnny doesn't learn to read as a child, he's likely to get plenty of on-the-job training later.

Occupations, professions and environments are in

such a state of continuous change that the individual who fails to read puts himself in a poor competitive position. I have never known any highly successful business or professional people who weren't avid readers. It's one characteristic common to every effective person I've known.

Effective people have long since learned that knowledge is power. They are also aware that to remain effective they must keep informed as to the changes and events of the world and their industry or profession, and adapt as necessary.

Obviously, the problem is not finding something to read. This is the age of information overload. There's too little time and too much printed matter vying for our attention. The most important key to reading effectiveness can be summed up in one word—*selectivity*. Effectiveness in reading, like everything else, consists of doing less better, rather than doing more or doing it faster. If you read at an average rate of two hundred fifty words per minute, knowing not to read that hundred-thousand-word book that just came in the mail will save you six hours and forty minutes of reading time. Through selective reading techniques, you can case the book and make a fairly rapid decision on whether or not to read it, or what parts to read. Here's how:

1. Always evaluate your professional reading in light of your goals. Before reading something ask yourself, "Is this likely to move me toward my goals?" If not, throw it out or send it on its way.

2. Look for logic, ideas and major points in reading material. Read the topic sentences of each paragraph. Anything of use? If not, jump to the next paragraph. If you're looking at a book, scan the information on the jacket, the table of contents, the preface, the index and

the author's credentials. You can quickly size up whether there is anything of use to you or not. If you see only a section or chapter of use, read it and put the book aside.

3. Reduce your reading load to the bare necessities. If you subscribe to professional or trade journals, cut them to a minimum. A lot of reading can be delegated to subordinates if you need to keep informed and don't have enough reading time. They in turn can underline key points or summarize articles for you, thus keeping you and themselves informed.

4. If you read a book or report that you have to refer to again, underline major points and make notes in the margin. When you have to refer to it later your rereading time will be a small fraction of your first time. In addition, being an active reader enhances your ability to remember key ideas.

5. Don't allow your reading to build up. Resolve to either read it by a certain date or discard it. Keeping informed doesn't mean reading last year's or last month's ideas today. Think of reading material much as you would think of a movie playing at a local theater. After a certain date it's gone, and if it's truly spectacular it will be around again.

6. Finally, you can increase your reading effectiveness by increasing your reading speed, although this isn't nearly as important as being selective. Rapid-reading courses abound, making phenomenal claims to reduce reading time the way microwave ovens reduce cooking time. Most people who claim to read at thousands of words per minute are in actuality skimming rather than doing comprehensive reading. Their ability to understand and retain what they read for a sustained period of time is

somewhat impaired. Nevertheless, most rapid-reading courses will make a significant improvement in your reading ability.

Some of the things taught in rapid-reading courses are things you can practice on your own. For example, take in a phrase at a time rather than a word at a time. Force yourself to scan more rapidly and take in larger eyefuls. Don't readread, just keep pressing on. It may seem awkward at first, but eventually your reading speed will increase.

Accepting the challenge to reduce paper work can enhance everyone's effectiveness. Generate as little paper as possible and arrange to shield yourself from all paper except that which is absolutely necessary. Be selective. Create positive habits for dealing with paper and increase your effectiveness with improved reading and writing skills. As long as you're in the midst of the paper blizzard, you'll never find yourself a place in the sun.

4

Working
with
Your Team

CHAPTER 9

Who Else
Can Do the Job?

*"He does the work of two men: Laurel
and Hardy."*

—*Anonymous*

Do you work long hours or find yourself taking work home? Do you find yourself doing routine jobs others could do or be trained to do? Do you have trouble completing important tasks on schedule because you are doing your job and someone else's? If you answered yes to any of those questions, then you are a likely victim of the do-it-yourself work tape discussed in Chapter 1.

As I pointed out earlier, there simply isn't enough time in one lifetime to do everything. However, there is enough time available to get everything done if you use that of others. Such is the nature of delegation—assigning to others tasks you want or need to get done.

In one sense, delegation is a cornerstone of urban living. We leave it to others to provide our transportation, grow and prepare our food, build and furnish our homes, educate our children and so on. How many people made it possible for you to obtain this book? I'm sure at least a few hundred. The same is true for your food, automobile, clothing and virtually everything else you obtain. We learned long ago that assigning jobs to specialists makes for a society that works less and accomplishes more.

Yet in our jobs and daily lives many of us don't use delegation to best advantage. We allow ourselves the liberty of performing many tasks whose completion is of little or no importance. Worse yet, we spend our time on jobs that could be more effectively done by others. As a result, less time is spent on the high-priority items that only we can do. Our effectiveness is severely diluted.

The history of delegation is documented as far back as the Book of Exodus in the Old Testament. After leading his people out of Egypt, Moses became a victim of the do-it-yourself myth. He insisted on personally deciding every controversy that arose among the people of Israel. His father-in-law, Jethro, realized that Moses was suffering from a bad case of overcommitment and recommended a plan for Moses to be more effective. First, educate the people in the law, and second, choose able men to act as rulers in more routine controversies. This would free Moses to allocate his time and energy on more important, long-range and nonroutine matters of governing. Thus, the Scripture states:

> Moses hearkened to the voice of his father-in-law and did all that he had said. And Moses chose able men out of all Israel, and made them heads over the people, rulers of thousands, rulers of hundreds, rulers of fifties, and rulers of tens. And they judged the people at all seasons; the hard causes they brought unto Moses, but every small matter they judged themselves.

188

So one of the most effective men in history made himself even more effective through delegation. Of course we have to take into account the fact that Moses had the original to-do and not-to-do list. And he didn't waste any paper either.

The ability to skillfully delegate tasks is one of the keys to success. Knowing what to do and what to assign is important for everyone, even those who don't have others working directly for them. We can all profit from delegation, be it at home or at work.

WHY DO MOST OF US DELEGATE LESS THAN WE SHOULD?

It Doesn't Occur to Us

All too often we are so caught up in the activities of doing that the thought of getting someone else to do the job simply doesn't cross our minds. Perhaps there are many jobs to be performed in our home or at work that others could be doing, but out of habit we simply go ahead and perform them. There is a simple antidote for this. Whenever you have a task to complete, ask yourself "Can someone else do this?" If so, then get someone else to do it. Find someone else to cut your grass or screen your mail and sort out the salient points for you. This practice gives you more time and energy to allocate on goals with the highest payoffs. It may cost you a few dollars to get your grass cut, but you can use that time toward embarking on a creative project or business deal that could earn you an unlimited amount of money. Time spent in creatively developing one good idea has a payoff far greater than fixing the toaster, cutting the grass or going through piles of junk mail. Whenever you can afford it, taking advantage of professional services frees you to allocate your time to the things you enjoy most. Doctors Meyer Friedman and Ray Rosenman put the idea nicely:

> Whenever you can save some of your time by offering money in its place, do so. Strangely, from their earliest beginnings men have always seemed quite happy to trade the very limited days of their lives for disks of copper, bronze, silver and gold.

We Believe It Is a Sign of Weakness

This irrational idea is probably a throwback to early childhood. As infants we come into the world totally helpless. Our lives are in a state of total delegation and survival is dependent on others' performing tasks for us. As we mature, the parental message to us is "Grow up, be strong and learn to take care of yourself. Grown-ups can do for themselves and babies can't." Like many outdated tapes this one plays on into our adult life.

The image of the totally self-sufficient person may have been valid in a rural society, but in twentieth-century urban living it is a total myth. As was pointed out earlier, we are all dependent on each other for our food, clothing, housing, protection and practically everything else in our present society. To delegate is anything but a sign of weakness. However, to not delegate is to ignore one of your most valuable assets.

We Believe It's Immoral

This concept is a byproduct of the work tapes. The reasoning goes something like this: "If we aren't anything tangible, then we aren't working hard, and everyone knows and believes in the virtues of hard work. Therefore, by delegating tasks, we fail to work hard and thus lead an immoral life." I won't insult your intelligence by refuting such idiocy.

Your morals are your business and I don't wish to instill you with any particular value system. As I said earlier, it's your life. However, all morality is based on two very simple principles: Don't hurt yourself, and don't hurt anyone else. If there is a way that delegation necessarily has to violate either of those principles, I fail to see it.

We Want to Do the Job Ourselves

Many of us fill up our days performing trivial time- and energy-consuming tasks that could easily be delegated. The reason given is usually "So what? I enjoy it." Unfortunately, the "enjoyment" of doing less important jobs is often an escape route from tackling more important ones that we know less about or that seem less pleasant. All that busywork gives us a feeling of accomplishment and quells any guilt or insecurity we feel about ignoring important tasks.

Horace, an aeronautical engineer promoted to supervisor, is a classic example. Because of Horace's high technical competence and performance, he was awarded a managerial position. Unfortunately, Horace refused to face his new managerial tasks and insisted on spending his time doing the comfortable and familiar. Within two weeks after moving into his new office, Horace had his old drawing board moved in. There he spent his days doing exactly what he had been working on in his old job while the supervisory responsibilities went neglected. As

191

expected, administrative problems piled up and Horace escaped each day at the drawing board, refusing to delegate his design work to engineers. Ultimately, Horace resigned and went to work as an engineer at a competing firm. Although he was bright, competent and a good worker, Horace was his own worst enemy.

Fear of Losing Control

An insecure manager is a common target for this delegation phobia. Such a person fears that if subordinates are trained to perform more duties, he will lose his job to one of them. Insecure men react similarly when their wives decide they want to work. "God forbid what may happen if Mary can support herself!"

Like most fears, the fear of losing control is without any real basis. Playing Big Daddy, Big Mama, Big Boss or Big anything is only holding back you and others from developing to your true potential. If you play such a role, sooner or later people will wise up to the game. And they will then ask themselves one simple question: "Who needs you?"

"I'm Too Busy to Delegate"

In many situations, delegation does take time to call, assign the job, sometimes train the person and check to see that the job was satisfactorily done. Like planning, delegating is initially time-consuming but in the final analysis a time- and energy-saver. Being too busy to delegate is like being too busy to plan. By not making the initial investment of time, you only increase your chances of becoming an ineffective wheel spinner.

"But I Can Do It Better and Faster"

Once again, the problem here is expediency in the short run at the expense of long-range effectiveness. By doing the job yourself, you are only insuring that you will have to do the job again when it reoccurs. This excuse also fails to take into account the need to develop the potential of others. This is rather important, particularly if you are leading an organization, be it a family, a department, a corporation or a religious group. If you hold a position of authority, one of your duties is to train others to be useful and productive members. By neglecting to delegate, you block their opportunity to learn and grow by doing.

"My Boss Won't Let Me Delegate"

It's very common for the one above you to insist that you personally attend to certain tasks rather than delegating them. For example, if you are a department manager, your boss might insist that you personally interview and recruit all of your employees rather than delegating the job to an assistant or the personnel department. Or if you are a housewife, your husband might insist that you personally cook all meals rather than hiring a housekeeper or frequently eating out. In either situation the problem is the same. You and your colleague have a misunderstanding over the most important aspects of your job.

If you can convince the boss that delegating will bring better results, then the problem is well on its way to being resolved. Perhaps you can convince your boss to let you try delegating a task for a trial period and see what happens. If the results are favorable, you can continue to delegate; if the results are unfavorable, your boss may have been right all along—it may be an important task that only you should do.

Fear of Being Disliked

Most of us will not admit to it, but the fear of being disliked by our subordinates is a very potent reason for not delegating. Fear strikes out when reality is the pitcher. The fact is, most people like to feel that they are valued by the organizations to which they belong. To make a contribution, they must be given something meaningful to do. By not delegating anything to them, you hinder their ability to make a greater contribution. Subordinates usually look upon skillful delegators much more favorably than they do those who insist on doing everything themselves.

Fear of Mistakes and Subsequent Criticism

Perfectionism can be a ticket to ineffectiveness. Very often the problem is with someone who will not tolerate any mistakes and thus is asfraid to delegate. "If I assign this job to Harvey, he won't do it without messing it up" and "They won't do it my way" are common statements of the perfectionist.

Another cause of perfectionism is that your boss or the organization is one that won't tolerate mistakes. A work climate where no one has the right to be wrong is one that stifles growth and effectiveness. When people are chastised and criticized for making mistakes they start thinking to themselves, "I can't be wrong if I don't do anything." Consequently, they do as little as possible in order to avoid making mistakes.

194

Delegatees Don't Want to Accept Responsibility

You assign someone a job and bingo, he drops it right back in your lap. Such a practice is called reverse delegation. You often find this if you try to delegate tasks in an intolerant work environment.

A mechanic, whom we shall call Joe, was a chronic reverse delegator. Joe had been with the same automobile dealership for almost fifteen years and was said by his supervisor to be one of his best engine repairmen. However, whenever Joe was assigned an engine to work on, he insisted on okaying every detail of the job with his supervisor.

A new supervisor came on the job and tried to encourage Joe to make decisions and be more autonomous. However, Joe would always reply, "You're the boss. I just work here and don't want any responsibility." When I got Joe by himself I asked him why he didn't want to take any responsibility. His answer was quite predictable—"because when I'm right nobody remembers, and when I'm wrong nobody forgets."

"No One Else Has the Experience or Competence"

If your help is incompetent, what are you paying them for? Even if you can't get rid of them, you still may be able to get someone else to do the job. Most of us tend to underrate what our spouse, children, colleagues or subordinates can do. The only way to find out is to give them the ball and let them run with it. It's also the only way they will get the necessary experience to become competent.

Doing Everything Makes You Feel Indispensable

Often our need to be needed is what stands between us and effectiveness. Doing everything yourself doesn't make you indispensable. The simple fact is that nothing will make you indispensable because no one is. Life was going on for centuries before you were born and will continue, we hope, for centuries after. If you are trying to prove your indispensability, be honest with yourself and stop indulging your ego with such nonsense. It's to your own benefit to accept reality rather than hide from it.

We Want the Admiration, Respect or Pity of Others

You can show your friends, relatives, subordinates and colleagues just what a hard-working, totally dedicated person you are. Unwillingness to delegate is a common trait among many harried workers. By not delegating, they present themselves with an impossible workload, which is just what they want. And all the ensuing whispers about what an overworked and dedicated person they are is exactly what they want. It's a terribly unhealthy ego trip, as well as a great excuse for poor work.

We Don't Understand the Situation

What is needed here is more information to familiarize you with the problem. Usually more information will give you enough insight to know who to ask for help.

STRATEGIES FOR DELEGATING EFFECTIVELY

The following set of ideas is aimed at helping you make better use of your opportunities to delegate.

1. Give the job to the person or organization that can do it best. Select the right person or persons and the battle is eighty percent won. In an employment situation we often confuse the best person for the job with the person who comes at the highest price. While it is true that you will often have to pay top dollar for an excellent job, paying top dollar doesn't guarantee you will get the right person. In his sixteenth-century classic *The Prince,* Machiavelli summed up the idea nicely when he wrote:

> I maintain, then, contrary to general opinion, that the sinews of war are not gold, but good soldiers; for gold alone will not procure good soldiers, but good soldiers will always procure gold.

A good modern-day example of this is the National Football League. Year after year certain teams finish high in the standings and some are considered dynasties. The secret is simple. The coaches, scouts and front-office personnel have the ability to pick winning players consistently. On the other hand, consistently losing teams have been known to spend small fortunes on talent only to end up with the same poor results.

Andrew Carnegie, who was rather good at procuring gold, put it this way: "Take away all our factories, our trades, our avenues of transportation, our money, but leave me our organization, and in four years, I will have re-established myself."

Most college coaches will tell you that their most important factor in winning is recruiting. Whether you're coaching a team, leading a platoon or running a business, the situation is the same in that you are getting things done through others. And the cardinal rule of delegation is that you can't expect winning results with losing players.

2. Make sure those doing the task have the right training and tools. I touched on the need for proper tools in Chapter 3. Obviously, if you are giving the job to others, it is now they who need the training and tools.

3. Take special care to clearly and accurately communicate the nature and scope of your delegation. If you don't take time to explain what you expect or if your delegatee doesn't ask, then odds are that you are both in for rough sailing. This is, of course, assuming that the delegatee hasn't done the job before.

In his book *Management,* Ross Webber points out that there are various degrees and styles of delegation. He then lists eight styles varying from very little delegation to complete and total delegation:

(1) Look into this problem. Give me all the facts. I will decide what to do.

(2) Let me know the alternatives available with the pros and cons of each. I will decide which to select.

(3) Recommend a course of action for my approval.

(4) Let me know what you intend to do. Delay action until I approve.

(5) Let me know what you intend to do. Do it unless I say not to.

(6) Take action. Let me know what you did. Let me know how it turns out.

(7) Take action. Communicate with me only if your action is unsuccessful.

(8) Take action. No further communication with me is necessary.*

*Ross A. Webber, *Management.* (Homewood, Ill.: Richard D. Irwin, 1975), p. 392.

Before delegating a job, make sure both you and the other person understand which of those styles you are using. It can save you a lot of future grief.

4. Give credit to those who do the job. Sincere recognition for a job well done is another key point that will increase your effectiveness in working through others. A former boss of mine who was quite effective once told me, "It's amazing what you can get done when you are willing to give someone else credit. All I do is hire people who are smarter than I, explain what I want done and then recognize them for the outstanding job they do."

I had the misfortune of working for someone else who used the opposite approach. Anytime someone did his job well, it was taken for granted or the boss patted himself on the back for being such a good manager. This boss always focused his attention on what wasn't getting done. The result was that not much got done. People were put on the defensive, morale was poor and everyone met only the maintenance requirements of their jobs.

Make the effort to recognize and give credit to someone who does good work. Recognizing and rewarding desirable behavior greatly increases the odds that it will be repeated in the future.

5. Help others work less and accomplish more. Giving people meaningless, make-work jobs is one sure way to raise their wrath and lower their willingness to cooperate. As a professor I frequently hear a few of my colleagues complaining about the unwillingness of students, secretaries and graduate assistants to cooperate. However, after seeing the work they assign I can understand why they get so little cooperation. They assign work in voluminous quantities and ninety percent of it is little more than trivia.

When you assign someone a task, make it worthy of their time and effort. Like you, they value their time and energy. Provide the support necessary to get the job done in the easiest way without sacrificing quality. Such an approach increases your chances of success as a delegator.

6. Put an end to reverse delegation. When you assign someone a task, there is no reason it has to come back to you like a boomerang. If you tolerate reverse delegation, then you aren't really delegating. When someone drops a problem back in your lap, tell them, "I gave you the job to do because I wanted to see how you would handle it." If they still wish to discuss matters with you, ask them to think of as many solutions to the problem as they can, put them in writing and choose what they believe is the best one. This will increase their decision-making skill and reduce the time you spend consulting with them. When they have formulated solutions to the problem, you then have the basis for an effective discussion.

7. Delegate the right to be different and wrong. Just because someone doesn't do the job your way doesn't mean he is any less capable. We would consider a coach odd, at best, if he insisted that a star left-handed quarterback throw with his right hand because the coach was right-handed. Yet how often do we insist that others "be reasonable and do it our way"?

Similarly, mistakes are a part of the learning process and should be expected and tolerated as long as people are willing to learn from them. I once heard of a manager who made each employee stand and tell of at least one mistake he had made that week. The manager reasoned that those who didn't have any mistakes to report likely weren't doing or trying enough things. It's an interesting thought. Life is, in one sense, a process of mistakes. I personally don't recommend such a practice. It's better to have people discuss their successes and to quietly tolerate intelligent mistakes.

8. Realize that delegation doesn't free you from responsibility. The classic illustration of that thought was the sign on Harry Truman's desk saying "The buck stops here." Even though you assign the job to someone else, you do not transfer your responsibility for seeing that the job gets done.

After World War II this concept was applied in the war crimes trials. High-level leaders were tried, imprisoned and executed for atrocities committed by subordinates even though it couldn't be proven that they had ordered them. The reasoning was that those having the final authority are ultimately responsible.

9. Assign tasks by requesting rather than ordering. We live in a free society where everyone has a choice. Others can do the job you want them to or tell you to go to hell. All of us like to think of ourselves as worthy of respect and courtesy. Consequently, how you go about assigning tasks is often as important as what you assign. There's a great deal of difference between "Mary, can you wrap up the Hobart report this week?" and "Mary, wrap up the Hobart report this week." It may not make any difference in whether or not the report gets done but the cumulative effect of behaving like an autocrat is sooner or later bound to take its toll. Resort to giving orders only when everything else fails. Courtesy and respect are contagious. In delegating, a little tact goes a long way.

10. Specify the conditions for satisfactory performance at the outset. Have you ever given someone a job to do

only to remark later, "This isn't what I wanted at all"? This can usually be avoided by taking the initial time to explain what you want done, how you want it done and when you want it done. It may also help to specify subgoals or request progress reports on long-term assignments.

In addition to communicating your expectations it is very useful to explain why the task is important, useful and necessary. Often the reasons for doing a job are not apparent to the one who has to do it. If you take the time to explain the job's importance, the odds are that those who have to do it will be better motivated.

11. Follow up. As long as you are responsible for a task, it is your job to insure that it's carried out. Thus, the final step in most delegation is to check on the performance of the work. Habitually delegating without following up invites problems. Follow-up questions to ask are: "Who did the job?" "How was it done?" "Was the work satisfactory?" "What can be done to do the job faster, easier and better in the future?"

Those are the basic ingredients for successful delegation. Skillfully delegating will give you more time to devote to your important tasks, your hobbies or whatever. It also can point the way to a less hassled life and improve your relationships with others. Such a small initial investment of time can give you a great payoff. What more can you ask for?

HOW YOUR SECRETARY CAN HELP YOU WORK LESS AND ACCOMPLISH MORE

A discussion of delegation wouldn't be complete without at least touching on the subject of secretaries. If you talk to the people who make things happen, be it in business, government or wherever, they are often quick to attribute a large amount of their success to the effective use of secretaries and administrative assistants. Competent, trustworthy secretaries are worth their weight in gold and then some. A president of a major manufacturing firm once told me that his personal secretary was the closest thing he had to an indispensable employee.

Unfortunately, many of us underestimate the true potential of secretaries. Many regard the secretary as a mindless individual who sits around and gossips until there is a letter to be typed or something needs to be filed. Such an attitude creates a tragic waste of human talent. The following is a list of things your secretary can do to enable you to increase your effectivess:

1. A good secretary can learn your principles of organization and see to it that you stay organized. He or she can keep your desk clean and see to it that the highest priority item on your to-do list is waiting on your desk first thing each morning.

2. Routine correspondence and decision making can be delegated to your secretary. You can draft answers to everyday queries received in your office as models for your secretary to follow. This frees you to work on nonroutine and nonrecurring types of problems.

3. Your secretary can keep your appointment schedule and act as a buffer to screen you from drop-in visitors and telephone calls, leaving you to work uninterrupted on important matters that are worthy of your concentration.

4. Similarly, a well-informed secretary can drastically cut your reading time by screening your mail and circling items worthy of your attention.

5. A personable secretary can serve as your ambassador of goodwill to all who come in contact with your office. You can also charge your secretary with reminding you to arrange for recognition of subordinates and customers on their birthdays, special events, Christmas and so on.

6. Given the opportunity, an intelligent and informed secretary can provide valuable assistance in the substantive part of your work, often supplying ideas concerning problems to be solved and decisions to be made that you can't procure yourself. If you are charged with writing a research report or preparing a budget, your secretary can locate and gather necessary information and digest it into a meaningful form ready for your use. And as a sounding board for your ideas, a secretary can keep you sharp and help you uncover any pitfalls or substantial oversights you may have made.

Guidelines for Secretarial Effectiveness

About secretaries, Oscar Wilde once wrote: "When I went to America I had two secretaries, one for autographs, the other for locks of hair. Within six months the one had died of writer's cramp, the other was completely bald."

While humorous, such an egotistical and exploitative approach to secretaries is exactly the opposite of what is needed to make the most of your secretarial resources. One fact many of us overlook is that a secretary is in a powerful position. A good and dedicated secretary can compensate for many of your shortcomings, and a poor or unmotivated one can greatly reduce your effectiveness.

With that in mind, here are some thoughts to help you get the most from working with your secretary:

1. Get the very best one you can. Don't hire some-one to take dictation, file and type. Get an alert, bright, educated person who is worthy of your time and trust. Look for a diamond in the rough. Often you will spot a talented, ambitious person whose only shortcoming is lack of training in management skills. You might consider hiring such a person and paying the cost of training. Business schools and universities have recognized the need to train secretaries in management as well as clerical skills.

2. Your secretary is a key member of your team. Never underestimate the power of a good secretary.

3. Keep your secretary informed of your goals, pri-orities and aspirations. This will enable him or her to organize your work for greatest effectiveness. Ask for ideas. Once your secretary feels confident of your sincere interest, there will be many thoughts forthcoming. In most large organizations, you will tend to find some of the best secretaries at the top levels. To be sure, some were hired at that level because of their proficiency. However, others are there because they climbed the ladder with their bosses. Their effort, no doubt, contributed greatly to their bosses' reaching the upper echelons.

4. Don't waste your secretary's time by putting him or her on hold while you fumble around for documents, addresses or telephone numbers. Such habits, along with assigning needless tasks, are great ways to alienate a valuable member of your team.

5. Give your secretary the authority to make deci-sions and solve problems. If he or she hasn't been given

such authority before, start with small, routine tasks, then gradually turn over more complex assignments. More often than not, you will be pleasantly surprised at what gets done.

6. Give your secretary all the support, recognition, respect and salary you can. According to an anonymous source, a secretary should have the following qualifications: "A diplomat's tact, a mule's endurance, a chameleon's effacement, a salesman's enthusiasm, the sun's punctuality, the speed of light, a sister's loyalty, a rhino's hide, an Einsteinian brain, a mother's sympathy and the patience of Job."

Anyone who has a first-class secretary will likely tell you that the above quote is an understatement of the person who runs his office.

CHAPTER 10

Keeping Communications Open

*"If only everyone talked the way we do in my
household. I mean . . . if only everyone . . .
like . . . talked . . . you know . . . the way
we do . . . right? It would be so much . . . like . . .
easier . . . you know . . . understand . . . right?"*

—*Robert Nordell*

Communication is the weak link in the chain of working
with others. In the past century, we have made superhuman technical advances in our ability to communicate
rapidly and to more people. We live in a society in which
we are continually bombarded by information. Yet while
more and more messages are being passed, it appears that
our ability to convey what we actually mean hasn't improved one bit. The infinite capacity of people to misunderstand each other makes our jobs and our lives far
more difficult than they have to be.

Consider the following hypothetical example of formal communication in an organization. A former student
of mine received this story while in the Army, further
source unknown.

A Colonel issued the following directive to the Executive Officer:

Tomorrow evening at approximately 2000 hours Halley's Comet will be visible in this area, an event which occurs only once every 75 years. Have the men to fall out in the battalion area in fatigues, and I will explain this rare phenomenon to them. In case of rain, we will not be able to see anything, so assemble the men in the theater and I will show films of it.

Executive Officer to the Company Comander:

By order of the Colonel, tomorrow at 2000 hours, Halley's Comet will appear above the battalion area. If it rains, fall the men out in fatigues; then march to the theater where the rare phenomenon will take place, something which occurs once every 75 years.

Company Commander to Lieutenant:

By order of the Colonel in Fatigues at 2000 hours tomorrow evening, the Phenomenal Halley's Comet will appear in the theater. In case of rain in the battalion area, the Colonel will give another order, something which occurs once every 75 years.

Lieutenant to Sergeant:

Tomorrow at 2000 hours, the Colonel will appear in the theater with Halley's Comet, something which happens every 75 years. If it rains, the Colonel will order the comet into the battalion area.

Sergeant to Squad:

When it rains tomorrow at 2000 hours the phenomenal 75-year-old General Halley, accompanied by the Colonel, will drive his Comet through the battalion area in his fatigues.

Mishaps such as the above happen every hour of every day in every conceivable type of organization. Whenever I give that example in seminars the candid response of many is "That sounds like where I work."

The problem of communication breakdowns will never be completely solved but it isn't totally hopeless either. Most of us do little to improve our ability to understand and be understood because we simply take communication for granted. Most everyone assumes himself to be at least a good communicator and places the burden of understanding on all those other people who obviously don't communicate as well. What an illusion that is!

With an understanding of some basic concepts of communication, we can begin to see some of the common ways that faulty communication occurs. And the first step toward resolving any type of problem is to recognize it. The first step to understanding poor communication is to realize that . . .

AS WE PERCEIVE, SO WE COMMUNICATE

Our ability to communicate is interwoven with our perceptions and thought processes. The result, as Lister Sinclair pointed out, is that we begin speaking as we think but end up thinking as we speak.

No man can completely understand beyond his own experiences. Someone may tell you, "I know just how you feel," but the fact is no one totally knows how anyone actually feels because no two people experience the exact same things. Your experiences, your sensory devices and your ability to think are uniquely yours. It is this tremendous difference in experience and perception that greatly hinders our ability to communicate.

Our ability to perceive is also governed by our needs. People generally see what they want to see. In the words of David Berlo, "Seek and ye shall find—whether it is there or not." Believe the party you are speaking to is

209

hostile, friendly, dull or whatever, and you will tend to see them that way. Poor children perceive a quarter as being larger than do affluent children. When we meet someone we perceive as important, we will tend to over-estimate his height. Thus our ability to accurately per-ceive reality and then communicate is greatly distorted by our needs.

In addition to being limited by our experiences and perceptive abilities, our ability to communicate is limited by our ability to encode or decode meanings into symbols. The fact is that what we experience cannot be transmitted as experience, but rather must be symbolically communi-cated.

Any type of communication involves a symbolic process. Something else must stand for what we are really trying to get across. Someone buys a Rolls Royce and parks it in his driveway as a symbol of wealth. Another person frowns to symbolize his displeasure. Still a third says "I love you" to someone else to symbolize his affec-tion for the other. As a small child you may have learned the expression "Sticks and stones may break my bones, but words can never hurt me." All this tells us is that words are merely symbols that are unto themselves harm-less. Yet do we really react to words as though they are mere symbols?

Consider the case of a twenty-six-year-old man who was a guest at his father-in-law's farm for dinner. The main course was supposed to be lamb. However, after dinner the father-in-law told his son-in-law that the main course had not been lamb, but was grilled dog. According to the Associated Press, upon hearing this the young man proceeded to strangle forty chickens, threaten to kill everyone in the house, cut the throats of three mules and three cows, break twelve hundred eggs and set the farmhouse and truck on fire.

The point is that it wasn't the consuming of the dog meat itself that sent the man on a rampage. It was only when he had been told he had eaten dog meat that he went berserk. It was the message rather than the experience that caused him to go bananas.

As S. I. Hayakawa pointed out, in one sense we all live in two worlds, the world of first-hand experience and the world of verbal descriptions. The world of experience is called the extensional world and the world of verbal descriptions the intensional world. The intensional world is a symbolic attempt to describe reality in the way a map describes a territory. However, very often maps are inaccurate and are always incomplete. It's when we react to the maps as if they *were* the territory that we often go awry. Such a confusion of words with reality represents one of several causes of poor communication and is known as . . .

The Intensional Orientation

If I were to blindfold you, put cold spaghetti in your mouth and was able to convince you I was feeding you worms, you would probably become ill. However, as in the story of the son-in-law, it isn't the real world but rather the verbal world that would cause your grief. However, if you realized that all I was giving you was cold spaghetti it probably wouldn't matter much what I said. In the first case, you would be behaving intensionally by reacting to the verbal world as if it were the real world. In the second case, you would check your experience with your taste buds—this is known as behaving extensionally.

The intensional orientation can cause us to waste a great deal of time and energy over matters that exist only in the mind, if at all. Relying on symbolic maps without checking out the territory can cause us a great deal of unnecessary grief.

The following fable appeared in the February 24, 1958, issue of *Newsweek* in an advertisement for Quaker State Metals Company. It provides an excellent example of how behaving intensionally can affect a business.

A Man Lived by the Side of the Road . . .
. . . and sold hot dogs.
He . . . had no radio.
He had trouble with his eyes, so he had no newspaper.
But he sold good hot dogs.
He put up a sign on the highway, telling how good they were.
He stood by the side of the road and cried: "Buy a hot dog, mister," and people bought.
He increased his meat and bun orders, and he bought a bigger store to take care of his trade.
He got his son home from college to help him. But then something happened.
His son said: "Father, haven't you been listening to the radio? There's a big depression on. The international situation is terrible, and the domestic situation is even worse."
Whereupon his father thought: "Well, my son has been to college. He listens to the radio and reads the papers, so he ought to know."
So, the father cut down his bun order, took down his advertising sign, and no longer bothered to stand on the highway to sell hot dogs.
His hot-dog sales fell almost overnight.
"You were right, son," the father said to the boy. "We are certainly in the middle of a great depression."

The One-Word One-Definition Fallacy

This is another cause of communication going astray. In Lewis Carroll's *Through the Looking-Glass,* Humpty Dumpty arrogantly says to Alice, "When I use a word, it means just what I choose it to mean, neither more nor less." While most of us seldom realize it, we generally operate much like Humpty Dumpty when it comes to communicating. The implicit assumption is that words mean the same thing to the other party as they mean to us. Yet for the five hundred most commonly used English words there is a total of over fourteen thousand dictionary definitions. It's easy to see why very often the words may come through but the meaning doesn't.

Puns and the double meanings of words are one basis on which much of our humor, both intentional and unintentional, is derived. For example, consider the sign hanging in a dry-cleaning establishment which read, "Drop your pants here—you will receive prompt attention." Better yet, consider the comment overheard by someone visiting the King Tut exhibit when it was in New Orleans: "They said they put the king's organs in this little box. How could they make an organ that small? I didn't know they had them back then. I didn't even know they had pianos."

Even better, consider these attempts by motorists to describe to their insurance companies what went wrong:

- Coming home, I drove into the wrong house and collided with a tree I don't have.
- I collided with a stationary truck coming the other way.

- A pedestrian hit me and went under my car.
- The guy was all over the road. I had to swerve a number of times before I hit him.
- In my attempt to kill a fly, I drove into a telephone pole.
- I had been driving my car for forty years when I fell asleep at the wheel and had an accident.
- I was on my way to the doctors with rear end trouble when my universal joint gave way causing me to have an accident.
- An invisible car came out of nowhere, struck my vehicle and vanished.
- The pedestrian had no idea which direction to go, so I ran over him.
- The telephone pole was approaching fast. I was attempting to swerve out of its path when it struck my front end.

When you stop and think about it, no word has exactly the same meaning to anyone. Words have multiple meanings. Word definitions change over time. Different regions use different words to describe the same things. Every word conjures up a different thought in someone's mind. When you become aware of the inadequacy of words, you start to wonder how anyone ever gets anything meaningfully communicated.

The Either-Or Trap

This is a problem when the structure of language lulls us into erroneous thinking. Consider the following statements:

- John is either married or single.

- Don is either a U.S. citizen or he isn't.
- Joe either graduated from college or he didn't.

Now consider the following additional statements:
- John is either intelligent or stupid.
- Don is either honest or dishonest.
- Joe is either competent or incompetent.

The first set of statements are legitimate dichotomies and the second set are false dichotomies. All of the first statements are valid depictions of reality, but what about the second set? The answers to those statements can't really be verified in simple yes-no, either-or, black-white terms. It's a matter of degree.

Unfortunately, the structure of our language makes no distinction between true and false dichotomies. Hence we often tend to think in simplistic terms such as rich-poor, sick-healthy, good-evil, beautiful-ugly, smart-dumb, true-false, right-wrong, guilty-innocent, war-peace, success-failure and so on. The vast middle ground where reality usually lies goes completely ignored.

Throughout our life, we are constantly conditioned to polarize our thinking. As you grew up you learned right answers, and all others were wrong. In competitive sports there is a winner and a loser. The courts decree a defendant guilty or not guilty. Elections usually culminate in a runoff between two people. And let's not forget the all-time favorite—there are two sides to every story.

The either-or trap is a favorite gimmick used by dictators and witch hunters. Hitler declared everyone in Germany was a Nazi or a lunatic or idiot. And if you think such tactics were limited to Nazi Germany, I need only remind you of Senator Joseph McCarthy and his communist witch hunts of the 1950s. Unfortunately, either-or thinking seems to be more the rule than the exception.

The I've-Said-It-All Myth

Bertrand Russell once remarked that "The demand for certainty is one that is natural to man, but is nevertheless an intellectual vice." All too often we speak with the unconscious assumption that we are totally correct and whatever we utter has thoroughly covered the subject. The next time you see two people engaged in a heated argument, notice the absolute finality with which they speak.

Of course, the fact is that it's impossible to say everything about anything. As was pointed out earlier, communicating means necessarily abstracting and abstracting means that certain things will be left out. Yet with our own limited perceptions and abstractions we try to ascertain how absolutely correct we are.

John G. Saxe wrote a poem about six blind scholars arguing over what an elephant is like. It's a beautiful illustration of the I've-said-it-all myth in action:

> It was six men of Indostan
>   To learning much inclined,
> Who went to see the elephant
>   Though all of them were blind
> That each by observation
>   Might satisfy his mind.
>
> The first approached the elephant
>   And happening to fall
> Against the broad and sturdy side,
>   At once began to bawl:

"Why, bless me! But the elephant
  Is very much like a wall!"

The second, feeling of the tusk,
  Cried: "Ho! what have we here
So very round and smooth and sharp?
  To me, 'tis very clear,
This wonder of an elephant
  Is very like a spear!"

The third approached the animal,
  And, happening to take
The squirming trunk within his hands
  Thus boldly up he spake:
"I see," quoth he, "the elephant
  Is very like a snake!"

The fourth reached out his eager hand
  And felt about the knee:
"What most this wondrous beast is like
  Is very plain," quoth he:
"Tis clear enough the elephant
  Is very like a tree!"

The fifth who chanced to touch the ear
  Said: "E'en the blindest man
Can tell what this resembles most—
  Deny the fact who can:
This marvel of an elephant
  Is very like a fan!"

The sixth no sooner had begun
  About the beast to grope
Than, seizing on the swinging tail
  That fell within his scope,
"I see," quoth he, "the elephant
  Is very like a rope!"

And so these men of Indostan
   Disputed loud and long,
Each in his own opinion
   Exceeding stiff and strong;
Though each was partly in the right
   And all were in the wrong.*

Confusing Our Inferences with Reality

This is another pattern in which faulty thinking results in poor communication. Consider the following hypothetical example. You are driving your car and are stopped at a stop sign at a busy intersection. On your left, you see a car approaching the intersection with his right turn signal on. You assume he is turning, proceed to cross the intersection and Bang! You hit him broadside. Later you find out his turn signal was on because he planned to turn into his driveway which was one hundred feet past the intersection.

Let's retrace your thought processes that led up to the accident. First, you received a message in the form of a turn signal. Then you inferred that the signal meant the other driver would turn at the intersection. You made this inference totally unaware that you were making one and proceeded to act on the inference as if it were reality. Consequently you crossed the intersection and paid the price.

We can't avoid inferences and make hundreds of them every day. The problems begin when we make them without recognizing that we are doing so. The consequences of such a mistake can range from humorous to

*"The Blind Men and the Elephant," John G. Saxe, *Interpretive Reading*, Lowrey and Johnson, eds. (New York: Appleton-Century, Inc., 1942), pp. 44–45.

fatal. Unfortunately, the nature of our language doesn't necessarily force us to distinguish between statements of inference and statements of observation. All too often we jump to erroneous conclusions on the basis of vague or incomplete information.

Alfred Korzybski, the father of general semantics, provided the following humorous tale of persons who allowed their inferences to lead them to erroneous conclusions:

> In a railroad compartment, an American grandmother with her young and attractive granddaughter, a Romanian officer, and a Nazi officer were the only occupants. The train was passing through a dark tunnel, and all that was heard was a loud kiss and a vigorous slap. After the train emerged from the tunnel, nobody spoke, but the grandmother was saying to herself, "What a fine girl I have raised. She will take care of herself. I am proud of her." The granddaughter was saying to herself, "Well, grandmother is old enough not to mind a little kiss. Besides, the fellows are nice. I am surprised what a hard wallop grandmother has." The Nazi officer was meditating, "How clever those Romanians are! They steal a kiss and have the other fellow slapped." The Romanian officer was chuckling to himself, "How smart I am! I kissed my own hand and slapped the Nazi."*

Labels and Stereotypes

These constitute another communication mishap that leads us astray. All of us tend to label, classify and

*Alfred Korzybski, "The Role of Language in the Perceptual Process," *Perception: An Approach to Personality*, Robert R. Blake and Glenn V. Ransey, eds. (New York: The Ronald Press Co., 1951), pp. 170–71.

stereotype each other after a brief encounter. Once we pigeonhole someone or get pigeonholed, the evaluation, be it ever so false, tends to stick. William Haney calls such a practice "hardening of the categories." All the common categories have their particular images associated with them. And each of us, with our own personal biases, form opinions of each other on the basis of stereotyping. We all laugh at Archie Bunker, but every man is in some sense at least equally biased.

Our culture and our educational system teach us to label and stereotype. Grouping persons and things according to similarity can have positive value. However, to be conscious only of similarities is to neglect the differences that exist in all of us.

Everyone stereotypes but no one likes to be stereotyped. Stop for a moment and write down the following things: your sex, your age, your race, your ethnic background, your religion, your education, your occupation, your marital states, your political affiliation, the region of the country you come from, your height and your weight. Take a moment to consider the stereotype labels that are attributed to those character traits you have listed. Of course, many if not all of the stereotypic patterns don't apply to you. But you can believe that many persons who know you believe the traits do indeed apply to you.

To summarize, stereotyping, the unawareness of our inferences, the belief in and craving for total certainty, either-or-thinking, the one-word one-meaning fallacy and confusing symbols with the reality they represent are some of the common ways in which communication breaks down. Add to this the fact that most of us blame each other for communication failures and it becomes obvious why misunderstandings are so prevalent.

STRATEGIES THAT WILL MAKE YOU A BETTER COMMUNICATOR

All of us are far from perfect communicators, but some of us are farther away from perfection than others. Even if you were a perfect communicator (whatever that might be) you would still find yourself beset with communication problems due to the fact that you would have to deal with all us imperfect communicators. Acknowledging and practicing the following guidelines will help to make you a more effective communicator.

1. Recognize the inadequacy of communication. By taking communication for granted we only increase the chances of greater misunderstanding. Communication seems so simple because we have been doing it longer than we can remember. However, doing it a long time and doing it well are not the same things. It's a complicated, symbolic, abstract process with an unlimited number of things that can go wrong—and that usually do. As Emerson wrote, "It is a luxury to be understood."

Communication may appear inadequate, but what's our choice? For better or worse it's all we've got. We simply have to be content with it while recognizing the fact that none of us will ever be totally understood.

2. Get extensional in your thinking. Remember that words are only symbols for reality in much the same way that maps represent territories. Frequently things are not what they appear to be.

Classic examples of this are statements we hear

today about salaries of professional athletes. We are quoted the current salary of a highly paid baseball player and someone remarks, "Gee whiz! Babe Ruth only made $80,000 a year in his heyday." Of course, when you take into account the income taxes today's player pays and deflate his salary to account for the shrinking of the dollar since Ruth's playing days, you find that Ruth actually had a great deal more purchasing power than today's stars. If you doubt the map, it always pays to check out the territory. Such a practice can save you a great deal of time and energy.

3. Listen and look for total meaning in someone's message. Don't just listen for words. They may not mean the same to you as they do to the other person. Look for gestures, expressions, the sender's posture and tone of voice. Likewise, be conscious of these things when you are the sender. Remember that it's not what you say but how you say it that really communicates your feelings.

4. Consider the source. Whenever evaluating a message, who said it is usually at least as important as what is said. The better you know your communicator, the more accurately you will be able to assess the message and his motives for sending it.

That sounds like an obvious recommendation, but it's one that is all too often ignored. For example, a colleague may openly criticize your work when the actual problem is that he feels threatened that your potential success will make him look bad. The local computer or photocopy sales representative may tell you that you need their latest in hardware when your present machines have you drowning in clutter and information overload. Or your stockbroker may incessantly call you with hot tips. Why shouldn't he? His commission is based on transactions. It's a good rule of thumb to remember that people will tend to tell you what they want you to hear. And what they want you to hear isn't always in your own best interest.

5. Tailor your message to your audience. Choose words, concepts and ideas that they can relate to based on their background and knowledge. How well you do this is fundamental to getting your message over.

6. Ask questions. Many of us are reluctant to ask questions of someone when we aren't sure what the person means. This is usually born out of our fear of appearing stupid. However, a lot of confusion can be nipped in the bud by simply asking someone to repeat or rephrase his statement. If you think you understand but want to be sure, paraphrase the message and let the sender verify that you do in fact understand his point. If someone refuses to tolerate intelligent questions, he may not be terribly certain of what he is saying. Which brings us to our next recommendation . . .

7. Know what you're talking about. The ability of people to pass comments, ideas and judgments on things that they are ignorant of or don't have the slightest understanding of abounds daily. Someone participating in a national poll was recently asked, "What do you think about cyclamates?" Her response was, "I think any two cyclamates who live together should get married."

You can save yourself and others a lot of future headaches by taking the time to get your facts straight and know something about what you are communicating about.

8. Be specific. Don't beat around the bush by speaking in vague generalities. If you make a general statement, have something specific to illustrate your point. Don't say,

"Foghorn is doing a lousy job as division sales manager." Instead say, "Foghorn's department has had high turnover, high absenteeism and a poor track record on sales ever since he took over last year"—and have the facts to back it up.

9. Communicate in simple, everyday language. The way we tend to assess someone's intelligence on the basis of the number of big words he uses never ceases to amaze me. To be sure, many professional and technical terms are worksavers that allow the professionals to communicate more rapidly with each other. However, a great deal of what we read in medical, legal, technical and academic documents is little more than the old professional snow-job game—If you can't dazzle them with brilliance, baffle them with bullshit. Have you ever tried to read your insurance policies, federal laws that govern you, or the act of sale for your house? Good luck. The purpose of a great deal of the jargon is to protect the future of experts rather than the consumer.

Here's something you can have fun with. It's called the "Systematic Buzz-Phrase Projector" and has been around for some time. It is believed to have originated in the Royal Canadian Air Force and consists of the following three columns of buzzwords:

COLUMN 1	COLUMN 2	COLUMN 3
0. integrated	0. management	0. options
1. total	1. organizational	1. flexibility
2. systematized	2. monitored	2. capability
3. parallel	3. reciprocal	3. mobility
4. functional	4. digital	4. programming
5. responsive	5. logic	5. concept
6. optical	6. transitional	6. time-phase

7. synchronized	7. incremental	7. projection
8. compatible	8. third-generation	8. hardware
9. balanced	9. policy	9. contingency

With those three columns, you're equipped to formulate your own buzzwords, designed to impress and confuse all you know. Just think of three digits at random (say 5, 8, 4), look up the corresponding buzzwords and presto! You now have "responsive third-generation programming." Eat your heart out, IBM!

The only problem with such communication is that it is mostly noncommunication. It's only useful for confusing others and impressing the gullible. The highly intelligent communicator is one who knows how to simplify and tailor his message for greatest understanding by the receiver.

If you want to embellish your messages in a smoke screen of double talk, so be it. Just be honest and ask yourself, "What am I really trying to get across?"

10. Don't be afraid to say "I don't know." All of us know terribly little about the world in which we live. The amount of knowledge that we don't know is infinitely larger than the amount of knowledge any one person does know. Neither you nor I have a corner on the knowledge market. So what's the big deal if someone asks you a question you honestly have no idea how to answer? Faking the answer only compounds the problems of ignorance.

11. Remember that anything that communicates *is* communication. A rumpled, smudged letter filled with errors tells you that the party sending it is somewhat less

than meticulous. Someone who fails to take care of his appearance or health tells you something about his self-image. Punctuality communicates. Body language communicates. Your tone of voice communicates. And silence communicates. Keep all of these factors in mind. You may be inadvertently sending wrong messages.

12. Spring the either-or trap. Most things in life don't fall into simple black and white categories. There are infinitely many shades of gray in between. There is a large middle ground between good and bad, honest and dishonest, success and failure and so on. Recognize it as such and think in terms of degrees of goodness, honesty, success and so on.

But a word of caution—there are legitimate dichotomies. Never let your boyfriend tell you he's a little bit married or your girlfriend tell you she's a little bit pregnant.

13. Realize that you can never say everything about anything. As Justice Louis Brandeis said, "Behind every argument is someone's ignorance." Anytime you communicate about anything, no matter how simple, you will leave something out. Due to our limited perceptive abilities, we will never know everything about anything. Bertrand Russell pointed out that our certainty varies inversely with knowledge. We will never have all the answers. Beware of those who believe they do. It's a sure sign of ignorance.

14. Give those you communicate with your undivided attention. Most of us can do only one thing at a time well. Shuffling papers, answering the telephone, staring out the window and tapping your pencil communicate a mood of indifference. If you don't want to talk to the

person, don't see him. If you do take the time to communicate with someone, give him the interest and attention that you would have him give you. Look him straight in the eye. If it bothers you to look him in the eye, look at the bridge of his nose (he won't be able to tell the difference). Listen attentively and contribute to the conversation when appropriate.

15. Don't interrupt the other person. This is a very quick way to put an end to meaningful communication. Your interruption tells the other party, "Please shut up—what I have to say is far more important!"

16. Communicate your ideas at the proper place and at the proper time for maximum useful impact. The Christmas party isn't the place to ask the boss for a raise or to evaluate your secretary's performance. The location and frame of mind that you and the other party are in have a great deal to do with how well your ideas will be received and exchanged.

17. Be aware of your inferences when you communicate. Did you personally observe what you are talking or writing about? If not, then to some degree you are dealing with an inference. Once you decide you are dealing with an inference, the problem is to assess the odds of its being valid. For example, we have all been taught that George Washington was the first President of the United States. That is a partial inference because we weren't around when it happened. However, the odds of its being true are extremely high. The statement that the sun will rise tomorrow is also an inference with extremely high odds. We can't avoid inferences, and we make a countless number of them every day. Life is a gamble. But all too often we bet on the sure thing that isn't really sure at all.

Successful gambling is usually the result of calculated risk-taking. Know your inferences and the odds of their validity before you speak.

18. Refrain from labeling, stereotyping and making sweeping generalizations about individuals or groups. By doing this, you only blind yourself to the uniqueness of each individual and thus hinder your ability to see him as he really is and communicate with him. Instead, make an effort to discover the uniqueness of each individual. The more you do this, the faster your stereotyping beliefs will tend to disintegrate.

Don't allow common stereotypes to dictate your own behavior. You don't have to love spaghetti because you are Italian or watermelon because you're black. Neither are you over the hill because you have reached a certain age. It's all a state of mind. Satchel Paige, who played professional baseball into his sixties, posed a most interesting question: "How old would you be if you didn't know how old you was?"

19. Don't overcommunicate. It's possible to say too much and, as a result, confuse the listener. Saying too much keeps your major points from standing out by surrounding them with excess verbiage. Worse yet, overcommunicators are just plain boring. Instead of saying: "I know you think you completely understand what I had to say, but I don't think you actually realize that what I had to say wasn't exactly what I meant" (thirty words), say: "I didn't mean what I said" (six words). Instead of saying: "In regard to the various and sundry reasons whereby you should wish to learn to make the most of your time and energy there are at least several good reasons among them" (thirty-one words), say: "There are several good reasons for managing your time and

energy" (eleven words). As James Russell Lowell said, "In general those who have nothing to say contrive to spend the longest time in doing it."

20. Realize that face-to-face communication is an ongoing two-way process that is the joint responsibility of both parties. There will always be communication errors but each error can be corrected in a give-and-take exchange. With regard to this, it's helpful to remember that when a message is sent there are at least six different messages present:

- What you mean to say
- What you actually say
- What the other person hears
- What the other person thinks he hears
- What the other person says
- What you think the other person says

21. Relax. A relaxed, open attitude will make people more receptive to your ideas and willing to share their ideas with you.

In summary, becoming a more effective communicator takes awareness of the problems followed by the effort to correct them. The information in this chapter can only help you to become more aware. The rest is up to you.

CHAPTER 11

Working With— Not Against

"A conscientious father was advising his about-to-be-married son: 'Cooperation is the foundation of a successful marriage. You must do things together. For instance, if your wife wants to go for a walk, go for a walk with her. If she wants to go to the movies, go to the movies with her. If she wants to do the dishes, do the dishes with her.'

"After listening dutifully, the son asked, 'Suppose she wants to mop the floor?'"

—Anonymous

If you want to work less and accomplish more, keep this simple point in mind: It's easier to work with people than it is to work against them. If we could harness the amount of time and energy that is wasted in needless conflicts between individuals, businesses, governments and nations, the achievements of mankind would increase at least a hundredfold. Unfortunately, man has always been a creature of conflict, and the idea of a conflict-free world is good for nothing more than daydreaming.

To be sure, not all conflict is bad or unnecessary. It's something we all experience within ourselves and with others as we mature. Many conflict and stress situations develop us into stronger and better human beings.

As a child, when you ran away from home, you may have felt torn between your need for security and your need to feel free. In your job, you may have experienced a conflict with your boss over what your most important tasks were. Hopefully, it was resolved by an exchange of ideas that enlightened both you and the boss and made both of you the better for it. In your marriage, you may experience a philosophical difference with your spouse over priorities in the family budget or the proper way to rear children. Such conflicts are a normal part of every-day living and their proper resolution can contribute to personal growth.

Unfortunately, a great deal of interpersonal conflict is a totally unproductive and unnecessary waste of time and energy. You may have six diplomas, a string of credentials, and an IQ of one hundred ninety to your credit. You may be one who knows the unknowable and can do the undoable. However, if your life is an endless series of personality conflicts, the chances of your achievement and success are greatly reduced. And the odds are that others will see to it that you have to work damned hard to achieve anything. Let's not have this happen to you.

This is not to say that you can expect to be re-warded strictly on the basis of your personal charm, for you won't. However, it is equally naive to believe that you will be rewarded or recognized strictly on the basis of merit. Just because you can dance well doesn't mean you'll get invited to the ball. All of us are social creatures and we rarely feel neutral about those with whom we work. The fact is that some people are extremely likable while others are about as endearing as surly porcupines.

CONFLICT-CREATING PERSONALITIES

It is often difficult to tell why one person is fond of another. However, it is usually quite obvious why unpopular people are unpopular.

Here are twelve prevalent personalities that are abrasive and obnoxious. Unfortunately, we all possess some of their traits.

The Critic

The world is literally full of critics. We even pay some of them to tell us what plays and movies to see, books to read and restaurants to visit. We pay others for constructive criticism to tell us what's wrong with our golf swing, or our business, or what to do about our neuroses. Professional and constructive critics perform a useful service and I have no qualms about them as long as they refrain from using their power to exploit others.

The critics I object to are the ones found on every street corner, in every office and often in the home. Unlike the professionals, they will give you their negative opinions on everything, whether you want to hear them or not. To the critic nothing anyone else does is better than mediocre. If only you hadn't made that stupid mistake, things would be just fine. He's the master of twenty-twenty hindsight, and about as welcome as the seventeen-year locusts.

As I pointed out earlier, most critics are frustrated doers who are controlled by a fear of failure. To focus his evaluations on himself would be much too painful, so the critic fills up his time evaluating you instead. That way he doesn't have time to do anything else and you get to profit from all of his brilliant insight about what's wrong with the world and you. Brendan Behan said it best: "Critics are like eunuchs in a harem: they know how it's done, they've seen it done every day, but they're unable to do it themselves."

Sooner or later you get tired of the critic and tell him where to get off. Usually he is quite offended and blames the conflict on you. After all, he was only trying to help!

The Aggressor

The aggressor pursues his goals with all the grace and tact of a white rhino in heat. He will likely be an advocate of the famous Lombardi philosophy—"Winning isn't everything. It's the only thing." Thus he concludes that life is one big Super Bowl and the key to winning is through a series of power sweeps. He is quick to identify himself with heroes such as Teddy Roosevelt, Patton and others famous for their "nobody gets in my way" attitude.

The aggressor often has a burning, almost insatiable desire to dominate and control others. Unfortunately for him, his brute-force tactics usually blow up in his face. People are generally reluctant to give power to those who appear threatening or who lust for power. The aggressor accomplishes only that which he can get done with force, usually after a great amount of struggle and confrontation with others. He sees himself as a conquering hero with a few battle scars from having fought the good fight. He likes to believe that nobody pushes him around. Others see him as an unnecessary annoyance with egg on his face. He hasn't yet learned the difference between aggressiveness and assertiveness.

The Gossip

"Pssst ... don't tell anybody, but Charlie's in trouble with the boss, the Jacksons' marriage is on the rocks and Harriet got that promotion so fast because she and the V.P. are having an affair. I also heard that Mabel missed work last week because she had an abortion and a rumor that George is a transvestite. Don't breathe this to a soul. Okay?"

The gossip fancies himself as the source of information. He knows the real story about what happened and will be happy to fill you in if you promise not to tell anyone. The only problem is that the gossip doesn't usually know the real story but rather some negative, half-baked rumor that is a product of someone's wishful thinking. As for confidentiality, Ben Franklin put it best: "Three people can keep a secret if two of them are dead."

Sooner or later the gossip chokes on his own grapevine. His information is not verifiable or turns out to be untrue. He is branded untrustworthy and people are fearful of sharing any type of information with him. The gossip finds himself on the outside looking in.

The Moralist

This is the guy who starts wars by taking it upon himself to tell other people how to live their lives. To the moralist, we live in a world of absolutes and he knows them all. He will tell you what's right, wrong, good, bad, pleasant and unpleasant with an air of complete certainty. And he'll be sure to tell you whether you want to hear him or not.

On the job the moralist is easy to identify. He's the one who tells you how to behave, how to dress, how to keep your desk, whom to associate with both on and off the job, and how to do your job. He is so absolutely convinced about the righteousness of his convictions that the idea of live and let live is totally off his map.

Most intelligent people are insulted by moralists. The subtle put-down is "You aren't capable of making your own decisions so I will make them for you. And if you don't follow my absolutely flawless advice, shame on you!"

The Martyr

Martyrs manipulate others by setting themselves up as sacrificial lambs. Like the moralist, the martyr's primary weapon is guilt. The difference is that the moralist tells you to feel guilty whereas the martyr wields guilt in a covert manner. By word or deed, the martyr lets you know that he has sacrificed his own needs for your benefit and that you are a selfish, inconsiderate slob if you won't do what he wants you to do.

As a hypothetical example of martyrdom in action, let's assume that you and I meet in a bookstore where you happen to be looking at this book and are trying to decide whether or not to buy it. After looking it over you decide you would rather spend your money elsewhere, and you put the book back on the shelf. Assuming the role of a martyr I would look terribly downtrodden and say to you, "That's okay, you don't have to buy it. Forget that I sacrificed the prime of my life to help people like you. Forget my poor eyesight that resulted from poring over the manuscript. You just don't understand how tough it is to write a book. Maybe someday when you write a book of your own, you'll know the agony of it all. Then you'll know how it feels to get rejections from publishers and flack from editors. Go ahead and put the book down. Forget about me."

Of course, in choosing to play the role of a martyr I left out a few details. First, I wrote the book because I wanted to. Second, I had a ball writing it. And third, it's a profit-making venture on the part of the publisher and myself.

Despite their cries of sacrifice, martyrs are the most selfish persons of all. Few of us can enjoy the benefits of someone else's self-denial. Of course the martyr isn't really sacrificing. He's getting some sort of perverse pleasure from playing the sacrificial-lamb game with you. Once you are aware of his game, you tend to ignore him and his cries of agony. Why shouldn't you? To pay attention to him is a needless waste of your time.

The Perfectionist

Perfectionism and its problems were discussed earlier. Have you ever known anyone who said, "I'm a perfectionist in everything I do"? Many of us believe that such a philosophy is the key to effective living, but such is not the case.

More often than not, the perfectionist wastes a great deal of his time and energy and, if you aren't careful, he will waste yours too. If you make the mistake of working with a perfectionist, you will frequently find yourself spending ninety percent of your time to get a one-percent increase in results.

I have three friends who spent over a year writing a three-thousand word article (that's a rate of about three words per person per day). One of them, a self-proclaimed perfectionist, kept rewriting, reviewing and critiquing the article and insisting his coauthors do the same. Despite all of their efforts at perfection, the article has yet to be published and has been rejected on several occasions. Many people who fancy themselves as perfectionists are wheel spinners who really accomplish little or nothing. As Nicholas Chamfort said, "Bachelors' wives and old maids' children are always perfect."

The Trivia Generator

The trivia generator keeps himself busy by keeping everyone else busy. In fact, busywork for you and himself is his only goal. He is the classic victim of the activity-means-productivity myth. No one has ever bothered to tell him that jumping around and splashing in the water doesn't mean you're swimming.

It's tough enough to be effective without the needless harassment of a make-work artist. Consequently, those who create superfluous tasks are very easy to dislike and can create a great deal of needless conflict.

The Short Fuse

The short fuse is the guy who reacts excessively and too quickly without stopping to reflect on a situation that he is confronted with. As a result he often complicates problems or creates unnecessary conflicts. To short fuse, every new problem is one of paramount urgency and importance. He is very high strung, intense and quick to lose his temper. Because he lacks perspective, short fuse spends most of his time solving unnecessary problems that he creates for himself and everyone else. He is quick to jump to conclusions on the basis of insufficient or inaccurate information and pays the high price of disharmony with his subordinates, boss, family and friends.

A department manager named Ben created a great deal of havoc with his steno pool. He decided one day that the stenos were taking five minutes too many on their coffee breaks and were wasting too much time talking with each other. He started spot-checking coffee breaks and severely reprimanded several stenos for what he termed "excessive chatter."

As a result, the stenographers got together and formed a work slowdown. They were very precise about their coffee breaks, they cut the conversation to a minimum and they spent fifty percent of their time looking busy. Morale in the steno pool declined, absenteeism increased and several stenos found jobs elsewhere. A clerical bottleneck was created and it was Ben's responsibility to solve it. He couldn't, and he was replaced.

The Bragger

Muhammad Ali has made a fortune by marketing himself to the public as a bragger. However, unless you want people to pay money to see you get your face reshaped, such a strategy will not likely work for you.

"Mine is better than yours" is the motto of the bragger and he takes pains to remind you of it at every opportunity. With absolutely no encouragement he will tell you about his new home, his expensive car, his great job or all the women who are after him. In truth, most braggers believe that theirs isn't as good as yours so they attempt to impress you by exaggerating their success.

This doesn't mean that you shouldn't have a strong

belief in your own abilities, for you are probably better than you give yourself credit for. However, so is the other guy. People who truly believe in themselves have little need to broadcast it to the world. The only things most braggers convince other people of is that their mouth is bigger, their self-image smaller and their presence irritating. As Wilson Mizner stated, "Don't talk about yourself; it will be done when you leave."

The Cynic

H. L. Mencken remarked that "A cynic is a man who, when he smells flowers, looks around for a coffin." Such is the nature of the man who always looks for the black lining. He is the ultimate kill-joy.

Do you have a new job? The company cynic will tell you how it has no future. Did you recently buy a new house? The neighborhood cynic will tell you that the neighborhood is declining. Are you contemplating marriage or having children? The family cynic will be happy to tell you about all the drudgeries of domesticity. Do you want to be happy? Tell the cynics to go take a walk and mind their own business.

Most cynics are little more than disillusioned idealists. Harry Emerson Fosdick gave some excellent advice: "Watch what people are cynical about, and one can often discover what they lack."

The Put-down Artist

Like the bragger, the put-down artist tries to enhance his stature. However, he operates on the erroneous assumption that putting others down builds him up. He hasn't yet learned that he is no more or no less a person for what other people do or have. Consequently, his attempts at self-enhancement are carried out at the expense of others. Such behavior accomplishes nothing and is only a needless waste of time.

Put-down artists are sometimes rather subtle in their approach and if you aren't careful you will often find yourself in the middle of one of their games. For example, one may ask you for advice and reject all of your solutions.

Consider the following dialogue between a sales representative and his boss.

REP: What in the world can I do to increase my sales?

BOSS: Have you considered making more calls in your territory?

REP: Yes, that appears to be a good idea, but the energy crisis makes that suggestion impossible. You know what a problem it is to get gas today [1974].

BOSS: Perhaps you can supplement your personal selling with long-distance phone calls.

REP: I've tried that but telephone calls don't do the trick. They lack the personal touch of face-to-face contact.

BOSS: Have you tried soliciting business through the mail?

REP: Even though it sounds good, that's the worst suggestion of all. Mail solicitations are seldom answered. Most of them end up in the trash can.

And so it goes—yes, but ... yes, but ... yes, but.... The sales representative doesn't want advice. He's trying to discount the boss. In another instance you may be given a decision to make where you will be damned if you do and damned if you don't.

A special case of put-down artistry is putting oneself down—the kick-me player. He will tell you about how stupid or irresponsible he is and then follow through with inaction to back up his statements. Consequently, he gets kicked out of a job, out of school or out of his marriage.

More frequently, however, the put-down artist aims his arrows of destruction at you and others. If you don't take pains to ignore these guys, they can waste a lot of your time and energy in needless bickering.

The Con Man

Although they come in various shapes and sizes, all con men show one thing—a lack of integrity. They take great pains to deceive others for their own personal benefit.

A guy who doesn't come off straight is most easily recognized by his ability to consistently say one thing and do another. Your boss tells you he always likes to promote from within, but fills vacant positions with outsiders. Your colleague tells you that nothing of consequence is on the agenda of the budget committee's meeting and there is no need to attend. Later you find they KO'ed your pet project so he could get the funding for his. Hypocrisy is the modus operandi of the con man.

Dealing with a con artist can be very tricky and time-consuming, especially when you don't recognize him as such. Listed below in the left-hand column are several common statements of the con man. In the right-hand column is the translation into layman's language.

Con Man Says:	Con Man Means:
1. I'm only trying to help you. Your welfare is all that matters.	1. You look like a real sucker. With a little luck, I can take you for all you're worth.
2. You can't trust anybody but me. It's a jungle out there, but I'll show you the ropes.	2. You'd be better off trusting almost anyone but me. Once we're in the jungle, you'll be at my mercy.
3. The trouble with you is you won't listen. Your stubbornness is going to lead to your undoing.	3. The trouble with you is I can't manipulate you. What are you, intelligent or something?

The detection of a con man is made by closing your ears and opening your eyes. Andrew Carnegie remarked, "As I grow older, I pay less attention to what men say. I just watch what they do." Such a practice can keep you from being exploited by those of questionable integrity.

So there you have the disruptive dozen. To be sure, you will always be plagued by them to some degree. However, by controlling your own behavior you can insure that the disruptive dozen will have a minimum impact on your own effectiveness. Coping with an abrasive personality is best handled by refusing to become one.

GUIDELINES FOR RESOLVING AND AVOIDING CONFLICT SITUATIONS

1. Make the effort to be an effective communicator. More often than not, conflicts are created because the parties involved don't understand each other's true meaning. Many of the recommendations in the preceding chap-

ter will help prevent unnecessary conflicts by insuring good communication.

2. Replace defensiveness with openness. If you stop and think about it, all of the disruptive dozen are basically defensive personalities. People behave in these fashions when they feel threatened. Consequently, the best way to discourage such behavior is to appear or behave in a nonthreatening manner. The more you are receptive and open to the opinions and feelings of others, the less inclined they will be to go on the defensive.

On the other hand, if others perceive you as hostile or threatening, they will often withhold telling you bad news that you should know until it's too late. Joseph Stalin is an excellent example. He signed a nonaggression pact with Nazi Germany which he held up as a monument to his wisdom. However, in 1939 Germany attacked the Soviet Union. Because of Stalin's hostile nature, his military advisors kept the information from him in fear that they might be punished for lying or failing. For days Stalin was led to believe that all was well while a real disaster was taking hold. His defensive nature kept others from sharing information with him that he needed to know as soon as possible.

Keeping a nondefensive, open posture can prevent minor problems from erupting into major catastrophes.

3. Present necessary criticism in a spirit of kindness, helpfulness and tact. On occasion, you will be faced with the necessity of pointing out mistakes or constructively critiquing the work or behavior of someone else. If improperly handled, this can be another fertile ground for needless conflict. Here are some ideas aimed at minimizing the chances of such a needless conflict.

First, choose a proper time and place, preferably a

private one. Never publicly criticize or ridicule someone. You will only put him on the defensive, and defensive people don't listen.

Assuming you have the proper place, don't jump directly into the criticism and lay it on the line. Start by paying the person a sincere compliment for something positive he has done. If you give him only criticism, he will feel totally unappreciated and will likely be reluctant to pay any attention to what you have to say.

Focus on the behavior that needs correcting, not on the person. To the extent that you can indirectly call attention to the problem, do so. For example, you may have had a similar problem or made a similar mistake and may wish to discuss what you did.

Once you begin to discuss the problem, be specific. Telling Jack that his report is all screwed up or Bill that he is doing a lousy job doesn't accomplish anything. If you want to help someone, point out specifically what needs to be corrected and recommend some possible alternatives.

End the discussion on a positive note. Express your willingness to help the person and your confidence that he can solve the problem if he wants to.

For example, if you assigned an employee to gather information and write a report for you and the report isn't adequate, the gist of your message might be: "Jack, you obviously spent a great deal of time and energy on this project and I sincerely appreciate what you've done. However, more data are needed in order to provide me with the information I need to make an intelligent decision. What I need is a greater emphasis on potential sales trends rather than dwelling on past data. I know our marketing research department has the necessary information to aid you in this task. Once you have combined this information with your talent for summarizing and report writing, I am confident that this will be a first-rate document."

In his book *Better Business Communication*, Dennis Murphy summarizes the difference between a bawling-out and a correction:

A Bawling-Out	A Correction
Is given in public and with anger.	Is given privately and with calmness.
Is seldom deserved or based on facts.	Is deserved on the basis of facts.
Combines sarcasm, threats, and profanity.	Uses straight talk and doesn't mince words.
Is given to humiliate and display authority.	Is given to improve and help the offender.
Destroys confidence, efficiency, and morale.	Builds initiative and encourages new effort.
Leaves everybody beaten and discouraged.	Leaves the worker anxious to improve.*

Finally, before criticizing someone else, make sure your own behavior is in order. As Louis Nizer wrote, "When a man points a finger at someone else, he should remember that four of his fingers are pointing at him."

4. Be assertive rather than aggressive. You can resolve conflicts and satisfy your own needs without dominating the other party or clubbing them into submission. Aggressive people are usually victims of the "some gotta win some gotta lose" myth. In most situations, it's possi-

*Dennis Murphy, *Better Business Communication* (New York: McGraw-Hill, 1957); p. 96.

ble to resolve conflicts and have everyone win to some degree.

Being assertive means expressing your feelings and satisfying your own needs in a pleasant and congenial manner. It means being responsible for your own feelings and assuming others are responsible for theirs. Assertive people are open and honest in their feelings and are free to confront others in a nonhostile way. It means saying yes when it is in your own best interests and no when it is not. And most of all it means not allowing yourself to be intimidated by the aggressive behavior of others. As Charlotte MacDonald wrote, "Aggressiveness is a weapon for battle; assertiveness is a skill that when practiced effectively helps everyone involved."

5. Mind your own business. Spreading hearsay about the business of others is ultimately never in your own best interest. In the course of our daily lives, a discussion about others is sure to arise and not all of it will be pleasant. Most gossip cannot be verified and is of no consequence anyway. By passing it along, you only brand yourself as party to the unsavory business of rumor spreading and such a practice can even get you sued for slander. As Mark Twain remarked, "A lie can travel half way around the world while the truth is putting on its shoes."

Some years back a college professor wrote a column in the campus newspaper charging members of the faculty with everything from gross negligence to exchanging grades for sexual favors from coeds. He labeled such a practice "an A for a lay." The community was amused, the parents angry, and the faculty enraged. Acting quite rationally, the university administration asked the professor to come forth with proof of his allegations. He didn't and was officially censured by the faculty senate for creating much ado about nothing. The following year he resigned from the university and left the academic life, much to the delight of most. All of his rumor spreading had only resulted in giving him a large black eye.

6. Live and let live. It has been said that one man's rights end where another man's nose begins. Such a philosophy makes a great deal of sense when it comes to conflict. The inability of people to tolerate and respect another person's values or lifestyle is the cause of many conflicts ranging from petty arguments to world wars.

Related to this is our neurotic need to find a scapegoat when things go wrong. Our laws have traditionally been based on someone always being at fault—hence the guilty party in court cases. John had the right of way; the accident wasn't his fault. Mary proved Joe deserted her; the failure of their marriage is Joe's fault.

This is not to say that we shouldn't be held responsible for our actions, for indeed we should. However, blaming is passing a moral judgment on others according to your own particular value system. You are in effect condemning them for not living up to your expectations, and such behavior breeds hostility and frustration that is guaranteed to hurt only you. Lyndon Johnson once said, "You can tell a man to go to hell, but it's pretty hard to make him go." Meanwhile you waste your time moralizing about this horrid person and the result is often more unnecessary conflict.

7. Keep your cool. When you run into a potential conflict situation, make delay your first strategy for avoiding it. For example, if someone makes a statement that you find offensive, your best initial response is to ask the person what he means. You may not have heard or

understood him correctly. If you decide you are being attacked, consider your alternatives. Is it really in your own best interests to retaliate in kind? It's usually just a waste of time. Very few things in life call for an instantaneous decision on your part, particularly when you are working with others. To the extent that you think about situations before reacting to them, you will succeed in avoiding unnecessary skirmishes.

8. Remember that arguing for the sake of arguing is a needless waste of time. Two people combating each other with their respective points of view is a great profile of two closed minds in action. By arguing with someone you have absolutely nothing to gain, and your time, energy and someone's friendship to lose.

If you want to convert someone to your way of thinking, I assure you that arguing will only make the other person cling more tenaciously to his old position. You must first be willing to listen to him and try to understand his point of view before he will consider listening to yours. Assuming he is willing to listen, try to indirectly guide him toward discovering your point of view rather than taking an authoritarian "that's the way it is" approach. As Blaise Pascal pointed out, "People are usually more convinced by reasons they discovered themselves than by those found by others."

9. Don't rain on the other guy's parade. All of us have achievements and possessions that we point to with pride and that mean a good deal to us. Such things might be our home, our job, our education, our family, our car, our trophies. Belittling or ridiculing someone else's achievements almost always guarantees needless conflict. Telling Joe that you don't like the color of the new car he just went in debt to acquire, or pointing out to Mary that

the cut of her new mink is last year's style are good ways to make enemies. To quote an anonymous source, "A wise monkey never monkeys with another monkey's monkey."

On the other hand, you will find people much more inclined to feel harmonious toward you if you make the effort to sincerely and openly compliment those things that they are proudest of. I'm not suggesting insincere flattery but honest and specific recognition. Don't just tell Joe you like his new car. Tell him what you like—the color, the style, the AM-FM stereo, the vinyl top or whatever. Eugene Benge wrote, "Learn to be an attention giver and the nicest things will happen to you. Getters don't get—givers get."

10. Don't be a prophet of gloom and doom. Life is filled with people who believe that the world is going to hell in a basket. If you are inclined to be such a person, I would suggest that you make it easy on yourself by keeping your pessimistic opinions under your hat. To those of us who enjoy life, your gloomy presence is about as welcome as a decaying mackerel.

We don't want to hear about Jack's skiing accident or the latest plane crash when we are preparing to fly to Aspen in the morning. We realize the risks and are prepared to take them. It's unfortunate that the predecessor in Joe's new job left because he had a nervous breakdown. However, constantly reminding Joe of that fact won't help him become one bit more effective. Therefore, as another antidote to unnecessary conflict, cheer up or shut up.

11. If there is a major ongoing, unavoidable conflict that is hindering the effectiveness of you or someone else, meet it head-on and discuss it with those involved.

Sweeping conflicts under the rug only insures that they will cause greater problems later on. Try and see the problem from the other person's frame of reference and he will be likely to reciprocate.

Carl Rogers suggests the following technique for resolving misunderstandings. Before either person can make a point or express his own opinion, he must first restate the previous position of the other party to the other party's satisfaction. Such a rule forces each person to listen to the other and adopt the other's frame of reference. The discussion tends to become less emotional and the parties find themselves doing more thinking and listening. The more rational people become, the greater are the chances for a mutually beneficial solution.

12. Refuse to involve yourself in the games of the critic, moralist, martyr, trivia generator, cynic or whoever tries to needlessly waste your time and energy. It takes two people to play these games and if you refuse to play the complementary role, they have no one to interact with. It's your life and if you want to be effective, you don't have the time or energy to devote to such counterproductive pastimes.

The best recipe for avoiding and resolving unnecessary conflicts was given by James B. Angell, a former president of the University of Michigan. When asked the secret of his success he replied, "Grow antennae, not horns."

CHAPTER 12

Summing Up: Are You Now Working Smart?

"Queer thing, but we think every other man's job is easier than our own. And the better he does it, the easier it looks."

—Eden Phillpotts

The purpose of this book has been to give you some simple, practical techniques for making the most of your time and energy. Those who work smart are not loafers looking for the easy out. Rather, they are people who make the most of their lives and thus create greater personal satisfaction for themselves and those they come in contact with. They are effective people.

These individuals possess no grand and glorious abilities that set them apart from the lot of humankind. They simply realize that the application of a few powerful ideas makes for an easier, more satisfying and productive life. In this final chapter, I would like to summarize some of the major ingredients necessary to increase your effectiveness. Much of this review is in a series of questions. I hope you will frequently refer to this chapter, especially if you find your effectiveness is less than satisfactory.

1. Do you focus on results? Effective people know it's more important to do the right job than to do the job right.

2. Are you willing to invest the work to get what you want out of life? Sometimes effectiveness means investing time and effort in projects whose rewards are in the distant future. However, effective people never underestimate the importance of enjoying today. While they are future oriented they also have the common sense to realize that there is no inherent incompatibility between enjoying today and building for a better tomorrow. The two ideas are viewed as complementary.

3. Have you searched your brain for any work tapes you may be playing? Ernest Hemingway once remarked, "The most essential gift for a good writer is a built-in shock-proof shit detector." It's also a necessary talent for those who want to avoid frustration and fatigue. Many of the dogmatic messages we have been taught about work are partial truths at best. When someone successful tells you how hard he worked, realize that one seldom asks a failure how hard he worked. Sweat, activity, efficiency hours and pressure are not linked to accomplishment in a predictable fashion. Every job is a unique one which will require various combinations of blood, sweat, tears, time and intelligence in order to be successfully completed. Remember that effectiveness is more of an art than a science, and constantly practice refining your skills.

4. Have you set your own goals and accepted total responsibility for achieving them? Goals are necessary for your happiness as well as being the vehicle that enables you to concentrate your time and energy most effectively. Set goals that are specific, challenging, realistic and mea-

surable. Be sure your goals are compatible with each other and give each one a deadline. Put your goals in writing, but consider them subject to revision and change.

When you set goals, set them on a lifetime, intermediate and daily basis. After setting goals, rank them in order of importance and tackle the top-priority projects first. Remember the 80/20 rule. Eighty percent of your effectiveness comes from achieving twenty percent of your goals.

5. Do you try to solve problems in a simple, rational way? Effective people appear to live a carefree, charmed existence but the fact is that they, like everyone else, encounter their share of life's problems. The difference between these people and others is that effective people realize that the number and severity of problems they have aren't as important as the way in which they are handled. They realize that becoming emotionally involved in a problem only lessens the chances of finding a satisfactory solution.

6. Do you distinguish between urgent problems and important ones? The tyranny of the urgent can wreck your effectiveness if allowed to reign unchecked. Remember, urgent things are seldom important and important things are seldom urgent.

7. Have you accounted for your use of time? Most time use is habit and we don't know how we spend our time until we try to keep track of it. Keeping a time log periodically can help us uncover and eliminate unproductive habits.

8. Do you keep a loose schedule? A good rule of thumb is never to schedule more than fifty percent of

your day. Murphy's Law can play havoc with tight schedules. Expect the unexpected.

Schedule most important tasks for prime time—the time when you work your best. Also set aside a period of each day for reflecting on who you are and what your goals are. Look for ways to make multiple use of time that has already been committed.

9. Do you know what not to do? Effectiveness doesn't result from doing more. It's the product of doing less better. The inability to say no is a great effectiveness killer. When you find it necessary to say no, do it promptly and politely to avoid raising unnecessary expectations. Don't feel you have to have a reason every time you refuse someone's request, but provide one if you deem it appropriate.

10. Before tackling a job, do you ask yourself, "Is this the best use of my time and energy?" If the answer is yes, equip yourself with the proper tools and complete the task. If the answer is no, get someone else to do the job or don't do it.

11. Are you a workaholic? Accept the fact that time away from the job is a necessary stimulus to greater creativity, satisfaction and effectiveness on the job.

12. Do you have a sound self-image? Do you know who you are? Recognize and accept your limitations and build on your strengths. You're better than you think.

Accept yourself unconditionally. It's the key to peace of mind and a peaceful mind is a more effective one.

The majority of people strive to improve their image in the eyes of others but the effective individual realizes that other-directedness isn't nearly as important as inner-directedness. The very essence of an effective person is doing things that make them feel good about themselves.

13. Do you put your own needs first? You can't help the poor by becoming one of them. Effective people are positively selfish. They refuse to be martyrs or self-sacrificers and give of themselves only when they have something meaningful to give. As a result, their help tends to be more abundant, effective, and oriented toward helping others to help themselves.

14. Do you accept the responsibility for your own feelings? Do you believe that you, like everyone else, make your own sunshine? Have you said good-bye to the time- and energy-robbing emotions of guilt and worry? When you feel anger, have you learned to use it positively to move you toward your goals?

An antidote to excessive anger is a well-developed sense of humor. Take your work seriously, but not yourself. When things get hectic, back off, look at things in perspective and learn to laugh at yourself. Ninety-nine percent of the time, things seem more important in the present than they actually are.

15. Do you build on your strengths? If you perform work that allows you to build on your strengths, you will perform with relative ease. Take a relaxed approach toward your work. Remember that how well you work is far more important than how hard you work.

16. Are you aware that being a perfectionist can cripple effectiveness? Somerset Maugham wrote, "Only a mediocre person is always at his best." Striving for perfection usually costs us more time than the increased benefits justify. Sometimes perfection is essential and on

those occasions, do your best to deliver it. However, most of the time it isn't necessary and wastes time that could be better spent elsewhere.

17. Do you have the courage to act and commit yourself to calculated risk-taking? As William Lyon Phelps wrote, "The fear of life is the favorite disease of the twentieth century." The courage to take calculated risks is essential. The only other alternative is a wasted life of inaction, immobilization and servitude to your fears. Better to feel sorry for the things you've done than to waste your life regretting missed opportunities.

Our culture is very security oriented and caution is the norm. However, to make the most of your life you must accept the fact that the only real security is that which comes from within. Despite what you have been told by your parents, teachers, spouse, clergyman, Uncle Sam, employer or insurance companies, no one ever gives anyone security. Life is a gamble from the cradle to the grave and the refusal to take risks makes for a life of mediocrity at best.

Measure success in terms of what you gain and not what you lose. You will have your share of adversities but these are experiences to learn from and not final acts. Mike Todd once remarked, "I've been broke many times but I've never been poor." Eighty percent of achievement is having the guts to try. Clementine Paddleford said, "Never grow a wishbone, daughter, where your backbone ought to be."

18. Have you bid farewell to procrastination? All of us will always be procrastinators to some degree. The important thing is to recognize it as a useless burden that must be minimized if you want to get things done with less effort.

19. Are you a frequent and skillful delegator? Smart workers aren't plagued by do-it-yourselfitis. They concentrate their time and energy performing the important tasks that only they can do. Anything that can be delegated is delegated.

Realize that there are many irrational temptations to avoid delegating, and work to overcome them. Accept the fact that others will make mistakes and do the job differently. Work at developing your delegating skills. It's quite an art.

20. Is your secretary given responsible, challenging assignments in addition to routine clerical tasks? An intelligent, competent secretary is a priceless aid to effectiveness. Get a good one and seek to develop his or her greatest potential. Many successful executives attribute much of their rise and fortune to the aid of competent and loyal secretaries who helped them climb the ladder of success. Keep them informed and reward their effectiveness with the support, salary and recognition they deserve.

21. Do you make a conscious effort to improve your ability to communicate? All too often the spoken, printed or written word is woefully inadequate, but it is all that we have. Keep in mind that all communication is a symbolic process that is interwoven with our thought process. We tend to start out speaking as we think but usually end up thinking as we speak.

When communicating with others, look for total meaning and be aware of the common types of communication breakdowns. Consider the source as much as the message. If you don't understand someone, don't be embarrassed to ask questions. Communicate your thoughts in specific, simple, everyday language.

22. Do you attempt to work with people rather than against them? Bertrand Russell once stated, "The only thing that will redeem mankind is cooperation." Some conflicts are necessary but most are needless wastes of time caused by poor communication.

Effective people resolve conflicts in a friendly, non-threatening manner. They are slow to criticize others and remain cool and unthreatened in the face of criticism. Their inner security and ability to focus on the important things in life provide them with the ability to avoid, resolve and tolerate needless conflicts.

Smart workers make life pleasant for themselves and those around them. They are perennial optimists in both word and deed. Because they like themselves, they find it easy to tolerate, accept and love the world and those around them.

23. Have you taken steps to minimize interruptions? All of us are subject to meetings, visitors and telephone calls which can derail our best-laid plans if we allow them to.

Avoid meetings like the plague. Don't be a habitual joiner. If you have to call a meeting, be sure it's a necessary one with a specific purpose and agenda. Time spent planning meetings and focusing on goals during the meeting can greatly reduce their time and cost.

Shield yourself from drop-in visitors. Schedule visiting hours and see drop-in visitors only in cases of emergency. Arrange appointments for necessary visitors and have others screened.

Use the telephone intelligently to save time rather than waste it. Know who your frequent callers are. Receive and make telephone calls at specified times. When you wish to work uninterrupted, have your calls taken by your secretary, an answering service or a telephone answering machine.

Get yourself a hideaway for serious, lengthy periods of uninterrupted work. Choose a quiet spot and let your whereabouts be known only to a privileged few.

24. Are you controlling and reducing your paper work or wallowing in it? Paper is here to stay but you don't have to let it clutter your life and smother your goals. If in doubt, throw it out. Never ask for anything on paper unless it's absolutely necessary. If you pick up a piece of paper, throw it away or do something to move it on its way. Never write when a telephone call or face-to-face contact will suffice. Paper is money.

When you have to write, do it with clarity, simplicity and naturalness. The key to being an effective reader is not to read faster but more selectively. Knowing what not to read is far more important than how rapidly you read.

25. Do you enjoy your work? Above all, remember what Senator Hubert Humphrey said: "Life is not to be endured but to be enjoyed." A life of satisfaction and happiness is what we all seek. However, we must have the good sense to realize that happiness doesn't result from inaction but rather from creative absorption.

Effective people have an intelligent type of persistence. They realize that most of us waste our time and energy by abandoning our goals too soon. Once these people attach themselves to a dream, they hang on for the ride and enjoy every minute of it. And they also realize, as an anonymous author wrote, "No age or time of life, no position or circumstance, has a monopoly on success. Any age is the right age to *start doing!*"

WORKING SMART

Working smart isn't a fantasy, but a reality within the grasp of all who choose to reach for it. The end of this book can mark the beginning for you—the beginning of a happier and more productive life through better use of your time and energy. I wish you every success.

Index

263

Index

Index

Index

Index